Supporting Children with Medical Conditions

Second edition

**Susan Coulter, Lesley Kynman,
Elizabeth Morling, Francesca M·
Rob Grayson and Jill Wing**

Routledge
Taylor & Francis Group

LONDON AND NEW YORK

nasen

Helping Everyone Achieve ■■■

Second edition published 2016
by Routledge
2 Park Square, Milton Park, Abingdon, Oxon OX14 4RN

and by Routledge
711 Third Avenue, New York, NY 10017

Routledge is an imprint of the Taylor & Francis Group, an informa business

First edition published 2004 by David Fulton Publishers

British Library Cataloguing in Publication Data
A catalogue record for this book is available from the British Library

Library of Congress Cataloging-in-Publication Data
Coulter, Susan.
Supporting children with medical conditions / Susan Coulter, Lesley Kynman, Elizabeth Morling, Francesca Murray, Rob Grayson, and Jill Wing. -- Second edition.
pages cm
Includes bibliographical references.
ISBN 978-1-138-91489-6 (hardback : alk. paper) -- ISBN 978-1-138-91491-9 (pbk. : alk. paper) -- ISBN 978-1-315-67979-2 (ebook) 1. Chronically ill children--Education--Great Britain. 2. Sick children--Education--Great Britain. 3. Special education--Great Britain. I. Kynman, Lesley. II. Morling, Elizabeth. III. Title.
LC4564.G7G73 2015
371.9--dc23
2015008224

ISBN: 978-1-138-91489-6 (hbk)
ISBN: 978-1-138-91491-9 (pbk)
ISBN: 978-1-315-67979-2 (ebk)

Typeset in Helvetica
by Fakenham Prepress Solutions, Fakenham, Norfolk NR21 8NN

FSC
www.fsc.org
MIX
Paper from
responsible sources
FSC® C013604

Printed and bound by CPI Group (UK) Ltd, Croydon, CR0 4YY

Contents

Section IV: Meeting the pupil's medical and physical needs

Section V: Access to the curriculum

Section VI: Developing skills for learning

Foreword

This book was initially produced in partnership with Hull City Council's Education Service for Physical Disability, the Special Needs Support Service and the Hull and District Cerebral Palsy Society. Guidance was also received from a number of health professionals within the Hull and East Riding Health Authority. It was written by:

Susan Coulter
Lesley Kynman
Elizabeth Morling
Francesca Murray.

It has now been updated to include reflect recent legislation and information about the conditions by:

Rob Grayson
Elizabeth Morling
Jill Wing.

With thanks to Lucy Riggs, RNMH Msc for her time for invaluable discussion and Daryl Perkins, Specialist Asthma Nurse for the use of the asthma policy.

The word child or pupil is used within the book but refers to children and young people as in the Special Educational Needs and Disability Code of Practice, 2014.

The term, school, is used but this encompasses early years settings and academies as well.

The definitions medical need and medical conditions are interchangeable within the book.

Introduction

This book is intended to give an overview of the considerations to be made when including a pupil with a medical condition/need (both terms are used within the book) into an early years setting, a school or an academy.

The legislation and guidance is mainly derived from the document 'Supporting pupils at school with medical conditions' (2014); schools may wish to consult the full document. This document outlines the responsibilities of the governing body in order to meet the needs of the pupil.

Definitions of the main medical conditions, experienced within school settings, are described. It is the responsibility of the school to ensure their information is up to date. Website addresses are given and the NHS information sites are also useful.

As emphasised in the above document, it is *essential* that the relevant medical professionals give advice and training to school staff before admitting a pupil with a medical condition.

The information included in the 'education implications' of the various medical conditions will allow schools to consider the support pupils will require linked to their medical needs.

Information and guidelines are included which relate to meeting the medical needs of the pupil, e.g. implications for staff supporting pupils, Individual Health Care Plans, the storage of medication.

This book also gives suggestions to allow pupils to have full access to the curriculum and to develop skills for learning.

Most importantly, the pupils' and their parents' perspectives are taken into consideration.

Section I
Legislation and guidance

1 Legislation and guidance

The majority of pupils with medical conditions are educated in their local school or academy. Their conditions are such that they can access the full curriculum when consideration is given to their medical needs. A small number of pupils who have medical needs may be educated in a special school environment but the medical condition is not usually their primary need.

Whilst the term 'medical condition' is used within the book, it is important to view the child as a child first not as a medical condition.

The document 'Supporting pupils at school with medical conditions' (2014) gives comprehensive statutory guidance and non-statutory advice for governing bodies and is referred to within this book.

Some pupils with a medical condition will also have a physical disability and are supported by legislation under the Equality Act 2010. The Act defines a person as being disabled if:

(a) they have a physical or mental impairment, and
(b) the impairment has a 'substantial' and 'long-term' negative effect on their ability to do normal daily activities.

Disability rights

It is against the law for a school or other education provider to treat disabled pupils/ students unfavourably. This includes:

- 'direct discrimination', e.g. refusing admission to a pupil because of a disability;
- 'indirect discrimination';
- 'discrimination arising from a disability', e.g. preventing a pupil from taking part in a school visit because of their disability;
- 'harassment', e.g. addressing a student inappropriately because they have not understood an instruction due to their disability;
- 'victimisation', suspending a disabled pupil because they have complained about harassment.

Reasonable adjustments

An educational provider has a duty to make 'reasonable adjustments' to ensure that disabled students are not discriminated against. These changes could include:

- *changes to physical features*, e.g. installing ramps to allow access to the building, classrooms;
- *providing extra support and aids*, e.g. specialist teaching and/or equipment such as appropriate seating, ICT equipment.

The 'Special educational needs and disability code of practice' (2015) states: "If children and young people with SEN or disabilities are to achieve their ambitions and the best possible educational and other outcomes ... local education, health and social care services should work together to ensure they get the right support" (p. 24).

It also stresses that "Where children and young people also have SEN, their provision should be planned and delivered in a co-ordinated way with the healthcare plan" (p. 94). It links with the statement from 'Supporting pupils at school with medical conditions': "Where the child has a special educational need identified in a statement or EHC plan, the individual healthcare plan should be linked to or become part of that statement or EHC plan" (2014, p. 9).

Teachers Standards

The following is adapted from the document 'Teachers Standards: Guidance for school leaders, school staff and governing bodies' (2011: 10–13):

A teacher must:

Set high expectations which inspire, motivate and challenge pupils:

- set goals that stretch and challenge pupils of all backgrounds, abilities and dispositions

Adapt teaching to respond to the strengths and needs of all pupils:

- know when and how to differentiate appropriately, using approaches which enable pupils to be taught effectively
- have a clear understanding of the needs of all pupils, including those with special educational needs; those of high ability; those with English as an additional language; those with disabilities; and be able to use and evaluate distinctive teaching approaches to engage and support them.

Make accurate and productive use of assessment:

- know and understand how to assess the relevant subject and curriculum areas, including statutory assessments

Fulfil wider professional responsibilities:

- deploy support staff effectively
- communicate effectively with parents with regard to pupils' achievements and wellbeing.

2 Governing body responsibilities

Section 100 of the Children and Families Act 2014 places a *duty* on governing bodies of maintained schools, proprietors of academies and management committees of Pupil Referral Units to make arrangements for supporting pupils at their school with medical conditions.

Governing bodies *must* ensure that the arrangements they put in place are sufficient to meet their statutory responsibilities and should ensure that policies, plans, procedures and systems are properly and effectively implemented.

Governing bodies should ensure that the arrangements they set up include details on how the school's policy will be implemented effectively, including a named person who has overall responsibility for policy implementation.

Children and young people with medical conditions are entitled to a full education and have the same rights of admission to school as other children. This means that no child with a medical condition should be denied admission.

Procedures to be followed when notification is received that a pupil has a medical condition:

> The governing body must ensure that arrangements are in place to support pupils with medical conditions. In doing so they should ensure that such children can access and enjoy the same opportunities at school as any other child.
> ('Supporting pupils at school with medical conditions', 2014)

In making their arrangements, governing bodies should ensure that:

- school leaders consult health and social care professionals, pupils and parents so that the needs of children with medical conditions are effectively supported;
- they are aware that many of the medical conditions that require support at school will affect the quality of life and may be life threatening, some will require more support than others;
- in cases such as a new diagnosis or children moving to a new school mid-term, every effort should be made for arrangements to be put in place within two weeks;
- the focus is on the needs of each individual child and how their medical condition impacts on their school life;
- an understanding of how medical conditions impact on a child's ability to learn, as well as increase their confidence and promote self-care;
- staff are properly trained to provide the support that pupils need;

- their arrangements give parents and pupils confidence in the school's ability to provide effective support for medical conditions in school;
- pupils' health is not put at risk from, for example, infectious diseases – they therefore do not have to accept a child in school at times where it would be detrimental to the health of that child, or others, to do so;
- the school's policy sets out clearly how staff will be supported in carrying out their role to support pupils with medical conditions, and how this will be reviewed – this should specify how training needs are assessed, and how and by whom training will be commissioned and provided;
- the school's policy is clear about the procedures to be followed for managing medicines;
- the school's policy covers arrangements for pupils who are competent to manage their own health needs and medicines;
- written records are kept of all medicines administered to pupils;
- the school's policy sets out what should happen in an emergency situation;
- pupils have full access to education, including school trips and physical education;
- risk assessments have been undertaken for school visits, holidays and other school activities outside of the normal timetable.

Governing bodies should ensure that the arrangements they set up include details on how the school's policy will be implemented effectively, including a named person who has overall responsibility for policy implementation. Policy details in respect of the above should include:

- who is responsible for ensuring that sufficient staff are suitably trained;
- a commitment that all relevant staff will be made aware of the child's condition;
- cover arrangements in case of staff absence or staff turnover to ensure someone is always available;
- briefing for supply teachers;
- induction arrangements for new staff;
- monitoring of Individual Health Care Plans.

Some children with medical conditions may be disabled. Where this is the case governing bodies must comply with their duties under the Equality Act 2010. Some may also have special educational needs (SEN) and may have a statement, or Education, Health and Care (EHC) plan which brings together health and social care needs, as well as their special educational provision.

All the above is contained within the document 'Supporting pupils at school with medical conditions' (2014). Further detailed reading is recommended.

Section II

Pupils and parents

3 Pupils' perspective

Pupils with long-term medical conditions may experience a number of emotional issues related to their condition:

- resentment, anger;
- embarrassment at some of the more obvious symptoms of their condition;
- dealing with a fluctuating condition, i.e. 'good days, bad days';
- reoccurrence/appearance of new symptoms;
- incidents of bullying or teasing;
- feelings connected to deterioration in their condition, e.g. fear, grief;
- disliking permanent medication and treatments;
- interruption of their school day to carry out treatments which can also restrict social interaction;
- interrupted schooling through hospitalisation and treatments;
- difficulty maintaining friendships due to the above.

Strategies to support the pupil

- Pupils with medical conditions will often be best placed to provide information about how their condition affects them.
- They should be fully involved in discussions about their medical support needs and contribute as much as possible to the development of, and comply with, their Individual Health Care Plan.
- Other pupils will often be sensitive to the needs of those with medical conditions and may be a support, either emotionally or physically.
- Discussion should take place with the pupil and their parents/carers as to how much knowledge should be given to other pupils about their condition. Information should be given in a sympathetic manner, in a way which would be supportive to the pupil, e.g. it may be useful for other pupils to have some understanding of epilepsy and what they should do if they observe a fellow pupil having a seizure.
- Management of personal health needs and medicines should be encouraged. Discussion with medical staff and parents will determine the pupil's competence to take responsibility for managing their own medicines and procedures. Self-medication should be reflected within Individual Health Care Plans.
- Independence should be encouraged by allowing pupils (where appropriate) to carry their own medicines and relevant devices or be able to access their medicines for self-medication quickly and easily. An appropriate level of supervision may be required.
- If it is not appropriate for a child to self-manage, then relevant staff should help to administer medicines and manage procedures for them.

- Pupils should learn to be self-limiting, e.g. taking breaks in PE lessons.
- If a pupil refuses to take medicine or carry out a necessary procedure, staff should not force them to do so, but follow the procedure agreed in the Individual Health Care Plan. Parents should be informed so that alternative options can be considered.
- They should have access to the foods or drinks necessary to maintain their health.
- Toilet breaks should be allowed with the pupil leaving the room in a dignified manner. Staff should agree plans, e.g. placing a coloured card on the desk, with the pupil to allow him/her to discreetly leave the room.
- It is essential that considerations are given to maintaining the pupil's dignity, e.g. if a pupil experiences a seizure whilst in school, screens to be put in place, other pupils instructed to leave the room.
- Pupils should not be sent home with issues related to their condition unless it is in the Individual Health Care Plan.
- Encourage peers to maintain contact with the pupil when a prolonged absence takes place through appropriate social media.
- Ensure that incidences of bullying or teasing do not take place, use 'Restorative Practice' if any issues should occur.
- Pupils should have an adult with whom they can discuss any concerns they may have about their condition, this may be the Teacher's Aide who carries out procedures. It may be necessary to identify a member of staff in a secondary school. The pupil may ask questions which are difficult to answer, home–school liaison will be important.
- Pupils may experience fluctuating conditions, i.e. 'good days, bad days', and school staff will need to be sensitive to this by watching for indicators and listening to pupils. On these days it may be necessary to lower expectations for work output, offer rest breaks etc.
- Ensure continuity of education through home education services, email interaction and/or extra support on return to school.
- Absences due to medical appointments should not penalise them or their classmates when attendance rewards are given.
- Provide alternative opportunities if some activities, e.g. certain sports, outdoor play, are not appropriate.
- Planning may be required for examinations, e.g. requirements for extra time to complete exams, use of rest periods.
- Access to after-school activities and off-site visits should be facilitated, appropriate support may be required.

Governing bodies should ensure that the school's policy covers arrangements to support pupils' needs ('Supporting pupils at school with medical conditions', 2014).

4 Parents' perspective

Parents of pupils with a significant medical condition will have many concerns regarding their child's safety and well-being at school.

These concerns may be that:

- their child's condition will be compromised through a lack of appropriate care;
- their condition may deteriorate when they attend school;
- school staff lack appropriate training to meet their needs;
- a person trained to carry out a procedure is absent or leaves the school.

The governing body should ensure that their arrangements give parents and pupils confidence in the school's ability to provide effective support.

Parents:

- may in some cases be the first to notify the school that their child has a medical condition;
- should provide the school with sufficient and up-to-date information about their child's medical needs;
- should be involved in the development and review of their child's Individual Health Care Plan, and may be involved in its drafting;
- should carry out any action they have agreed to as part of its implementation, e.g. provide medicines and equipment;
- ensure they or another nominated adult are contactable at all times.

Parents should not:

- be required or feel obliged to attend school to administer medicine or provide medical support, including toileting issues;
- be obliged to forfeit their work because the school fails to meet their child's needs;
- be expected to collect their child from school due to their medical condition unless it is stated in the Individual Health Care Plan.

Parents should enjoy a good working relationship with their child's school. They should know who to contact in school if they have any issues to discuss.

Section III

Medical conditions and possible educational implications

5   Anaphylactic shock (anaphylaxis)

Definition

Anaphylaxis is an acute allergic reaction requiring immediate medical attention.

Cause

It is most commonly triggered by substances to which the pupil is sensitive, e.g. nuts, eggs, milk, shellfish, certain drugs, venom from stinging insects.

Symptoms

Symptoms will vary from individual to individual and will depend on what type of contact there has been with the substance causing the allergic reaction.

Symptoms can include:

- itching;
- strange metallic taste in the mouth;
- sensation of burning or itching of the tongue, lips, throat;
- swelling of the face, lips, tongue with or without difficulty in swallowing;
- skin blotches;
- generalised flushing of the skin;
- abdominal cramps or nausea;
- increased heart rate;
- difficulty in breathing;
- sudden feeling of weakness (dizziness/fainting);
- collapse;
- unconsciousness.

Few pupils would experience all these symptoms.

Treatment

- Avoid substances which are known to cause a reaction.
- Use of Epipen (adrenaline) to reverse the reaction.

For further information contact:

The Anaphylaxis Campaign PO Box 275
Farnborough GU14 7SX

Tel: 01252 542029   www.anaphylaxis.org.uk

Educational implications

Staff training and administrative issues

'Supporting pupils at school with medical conditions' (2014) provides the legal framework that schools are required to work within. It contains advice and pro formas for school use.

- Medical training should be arranged for staff who have volunteered to administer medication in an emergency. This is usually in the form of Epipen.
- A clear procedure should be established for summoning an ambulance in an emergency.
- A foolproof mechanism should be established for the sharing of information with all staff who come into contact with the pupil.

Food management issues

- School meals – the catering supervisor needs to be aware of the pupil's requirements in relation to the menu. A packed lunch provided by the family may be preferable to a school meal.
- Snacks and treats in the classroom and playground – staff and pupils should be made aware that some pupils may not be able to share such treats.
- It may be necessary for some foods to be refused in school, if a pupil has a severe reaction to a particular food.
- Science and food technology experiments with food – these curriculum areas may cause difficulty for the pupil who is at risk of anaphylaxis. Suitable alternative arrangements should be made.

Individual Health Care Plan

The Individual Health Care Plan should be drawn up with the parents and school nurse. The following points should be considered:

- definition of the allergy;
- emergency procedure to be followed;
- treatment;
- food management;
- precautionary measures;
- staff training;
- staff indemnity;
- parental consent and agreement.

See 'Individual Health Care Plans' (pages 91–4) for full details.

6 Arthrogryposis

Definition

Arthrogryposis or Arthrogryposis Multiplex Congenita describes a baby born with multiple joint contractures (a contracture is a limitation in the range of movement of a joint). It covers a wide range of conditions, Amyoplasia being the most common form. This is not a hereditary condition but Distal Arthrogryposis has a genetic basis. The incidence of Arthrogryposis is 1 in 10,000 births.

Children with arthrogryposis may be characterised by the internal rotation of the hands, sloping shoulders and long, tapering fingers; however, the positions of feet, knees and hips are variable. In some children only two or three joints are affected, but in others all joints, including the spine and jaw, are affected. Most children will be within the normal range of cognitive ability.

Causes

A number of factors can affect the normal development of the joint and cause the fixation:

- muscle defects caused by the failure of muscles to form or function normally in the womb or by a degenerative process taking place at this time;
- abnormal connective tissue or joints causing limited movement;
- a neurological deficit caused by absent, abnormal or malfunctioning nerves;
- insufficient space in the womb for the foetus to move as a result of an abnormal womb shape, insufficient fluid or more than one developing foetus.

Treatment

- Early diagnosis is very important to enable treatment to start as soon as possible.
- Physiotherapy should start immediately to develop a programme of passive stretching combined with the use of splints.
- Serial plasters and corrective surgery can complement physiotherapy as the child grows.
- Lightweight orthoses may help standing and walking.
- Improvement of hand function is sometimes achieved through surgical intervention.
- Many children improvise and learn ways to overcome their own difficulties.

Educational implications

As with all medical conditions the severity of this condition can vary. Some pupils remain ambulant throughout their school days whilst others may require a wheelchair to aid mobility. It may be necessary to consider the following points when planning to include a pupil with arthrogryposis:

- plan classroom allocation taking restricted mobility into account, e.g. registration rooms on the ground floor;
- be aware that the pupil may have difficulty in climbing stairs;
- the pupil is likely to have difficulty sitting on the floor during carpet time and assemblies;
- PE lessons may require differentiation, consult with the occupational therapist and physiotherapist for advice;
- a physical management routine may need to be incorporated in the school day – consider by whom, where and when this will be implemented;
- manipulation of standard classroom equipment can be difficult if arms and hands are affected;
- limited recording abilities may necessitate use of specialised fine motor equipment and the early introduction to word processing skills;
- provide ICT equipment for recording work;
- reorganise positioning of equipment in the classroom to aid independent access;
- support the pupil in organisation of their personal effects, such as school bag;
- facilitate disabled toilet access with support if required;
- carefully consider arrangements for out-of-school visits and work experience placements;
- investigate home/school transport if necessary.

7　Asthma

Definition

- Asthma is a common condition which affects the airways in the lungs.
- Symptoms occur in response to exposure to a trigger, e.g. pollen, dust, smoke, exercise.
- Symptoms include cough, wheeze, chest tightness and breathlessness. Symptoms are usually easily reversible by use of a reliever inhaler.
- Sufferers may experience an acute episode requiring rapid medical or hospital treatment.

Record keeping

- Pupils with asthma should be named in an 'Asthma Register', for all school staff.
- Updated at least annually or more frequently, using parental information.

Medication

- Only reliever inhalers (usually blue) should be kept in school.
- An emergency inhaler should be kept centrally (guidance in 'Supporting pupils at school with medical needs', 2014). To obtain an emergency inhaler and spacer write to a local pharmacy, on headed notepaper (signed by the head teacher) requesting the purchase of a Ventolin / Salbutamol Metered Dose Inhaler and a Volumatic Spacer (with mask).

Access

- Immediate access to reliever inhaler is vital.
- Inhalers should not be stored in the school office or similar as this will not allow quick enough access in an emergency.

Recommendations

Key Stage 1

- The pupil's inhaler must be kept wherever he/she is at any time e.g. class, hall, playground etc.
- Children aged 7 years and over who are considered sufficiently mature are encouraged to carry their own inhaler (at the discretion of the parent/carer and teacher).

Key Stage 2, 3 and 4

- Pupils should carry their own inhalers with them at all times (further consideration should be made for a pupil with SEN).
- A spare inhaler should be kept for use if the original runs out or is lost.

General

- Pupils who are able to identify the need to use their medication should be allowed to do so as and when they feel it is necessary.
- Pupils should not be taking Ventolin every break/lunch time 'just in case' of symptoms.
- Follow the Individual Heath Care Plan.

Storage of inhalers

The following good practice guidelines for the storage of inhalers will be followed:

1. Inhalers will *NEVER* be locked away or kept in the school office.
2. All pupils with asthma will have rapid access to their inhalers as soon as they need them.
3. Devices will always be taken with the pupil when moving out of the classroom for lessons, trips or activities.

N.B. In the unlikely event of another pupil using someone else's blue inhaler, there is little chance of harm. The drug in reliever inhalers is very safe and overdose is very unlikely.

Colds/Viruses

- A pupil with a cold may need regular Ventolin for a few days.
- The blue inhaler may be needed every lunchtime for approximately one week. The number of puffs advised by the parent/carer; anything between two and eight puffs.
- This does not replace using the inhaler as and when needed – it is in addition to this.

Physical education

- Pupils with asthma are encouraged to participate fully.
- Symptoms of asthma are often brought on by exercise. The pupil's labelled inhaler must be available at the site of the lesson.
- Potent triggers for asthma are, e.g., cross-country running and field activities. If it is known that an activity will induce symptoms, the reliever inhaler should be used prior to exercise and carried with the pupil. Warm up prior to exercise and cool down after are important.

School trips/Residential visits

- No pupil can be denied a part in school trips/residential visits because of asthma, unless so advised by their GP or consultant.
- The reliever inhaler should be available throughout the trip, carried either by the pupil or the supervising adult in the case of Key Stage 1 pupils.

- For residential visits, staff must be trained in the use of regular controller treatments, as well as emergency management.
- Appropriate contact numbers must be taken.

Training

On a bi-annual basis, *all* staff should receive training on signs and symptoms of asthma and how to treat it.

Asthma UK has a downloadable 'My Asthma Plan' to support pupils.

For further information contact:

Asthma UK
www.asthma.org.uk

Display the emergency procedure on the following page in the staff room, office, hall, classroom where there is a pupil with asthma.

Managing an asthma attack

Signs of asthma attack

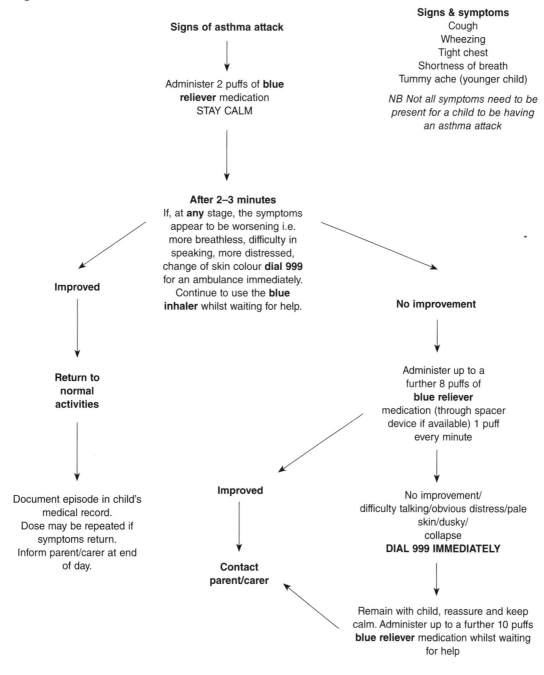

Signs of asthma attack

↓

Administer 2 puffs of **blue reliever** medication
STAY CALM

↓

Signs & symptoms
Cough
Wheezing
Tight chest
Shortness of breath
Tummy ache (younger child)

NB Not all symptoms need to be present for a child to be having an asthma attack

After 2–3 minutes
If, at **any** stage, the symptoms appear to be worsening i.e. more breathless, difficulty in speaking, more distressed, change of skin colour **dial 999** for an ambulance immediately. Continue to use the **blue inhaler** whilst waiting for help.

Improved

↓

Return to normal activities

↓

Document episode in child's medical record.
Dose may be repeated if symptoms return.
Inform parent/carer at end of day.

No improvement

↓

Administer up to a further 8 puffs of **blue reliever** medication (through spacer device if available) 1 puff every minute

Improved

↓

Contact parent/carer

No improvement/ difficulty talking/obvious distress/pale skin/dusky/ collapse
DIAL 999 IMMEDIATELY

↓

Remain with child, reassure and keep calm. Administer up to a further 10 puffs **blue reliever** medication whilst waiting for help

8   Brittle bone disease (osteogenesis imperfecta)

Definition

There are four types of osteogenesis imperfecta:

- **Type I** is a milder condition but bones fracture easily and very blue/grey sclera (whites of the eyes).
- **Type II** causes very severe fractures resulting in stillborn babies or death within the first few weeks of life.
- **Type III** is severe, although not life-threatening. Bones fracture easily, bone deformity, short stature and possible respiratory problems.
- **Type IV** is as Type I without sclera.

Associated problems may be:

- ✔ muscle weakness;
- ✔ fragile teeth;
- ✔ fatigue;
- ✔ bruising easily;
- ✔ lax joints;
- ✔ short stature;
- ✔ scoliosis.

Other less common causes of brittle bone disease include osteopetrosis, hypophosphatasia, fibrous dysplasia (Albright syndrome) and ideopathic juvenile osteoporosis. Temporary brittle bone disease may cause fractures in the first year of life and improve later.

Treatment

There is no cure for brittle bone diseases. Treatment is aimed at increasing overall bone strength.

- Fractures are treated as they occur.
- Plaster casts may be used.
- Physiotherapy will be necessary to reduce the impact of long-term damage.
- In severe cases bones are surgically corrected and rods inserted within the bones.

For further information contact:

Brittle Bone Society
Tel: 01382 204446   email: bbs@brittlebone.org   www.brittlebone.org

Educational implications

Mobility in and around the school site

Pupils are vulnerable to knocks and bumps that could result in fractures. The pupils and the school need to develop strategies to minimise the risk. Consider:

- supervision of movement at busy times, e.g. change of lesson;
- timing of movement between lessons (leave before or after the other pupils);
- timing of homework instructions if the pupil leaves early;
- finding a quiet, 'safe', social area for use at breaks;
- possible oversight at break if the pupil does not want to stay inside;
- moving the pupil's belongings between lessons.

Written work

- The effects of multiple fractures and lax joints can make writing difficult.
- Occupational therapy (OT) input can advise on seating and positioning.
- The pupil's hands may tire quickly and, therefore, writing may be slow.
- Use of ICT equipment where it may be helpful in some cases.
- Use of a scribe if fractures occur.
- Provide an additional set of books for use at home, to cut down on the weight carried by the pupil.

Art/D&T/Science

- Pupils are rarely static in these lessons. Support may be required to monitor the physical environment and minimise movement around the classroom.
- Care should be taken with regard to weight when handling equipment.

PE

- Most mainstream activities will be unsuitable.
- Parents and medical staff will advise accordingly.
- Swimming is often recommended.

Other considerations

- Toilet arrangements – pupils may need to use a specialist facility to avoid potential hazards within a communal toilet. Pupils with restricted growth, particularly short arms, may require assistance with cleansing.
- Consider the position within the classroom in relation to ease of access.
- Examinations – special arrangements may be required, e.g. rest breaks, use of ICT.

- Protection and over protection – be aware of the tendency to over protect these pupils. Ensure the pupils are given opportunities for social interaction.
- Communication – consider how pupils could contact support staff for assistance, when required out of 'timetabled' time (phone/bleep/walkie talkie).
- Autonomy – encourage the pupils to make decisions themselves.

Raising awareness of the pupil's condition

- Accurate information should be shared with all staff.
- Emergency routines via Individual Health Care Plans should be agreed.
- The pupil's permission should be obtained, to explain the condition to other pupils.

9 Cerebral palsy

Definition

Cerebral palsy is caused by a problem in the parts of the brain which control muscles. The term 'cerebral palsy' is a diagnosis that covers a wide range of ability and need. Some pupils with cerebral palsy may be of average or above average ability. They may have physical impairments affecting mobility and co-ordination; speech, chewing and swallowing; sensory impairments such as vision and hearing difficulties. There may be accompanying epilepsy. Other pupils may have moderate to severe learning difficulties accompanied by a range of physical impairments.

- **Spastic cerebral palsy** means that muscles are stiff and difficult to control. Within this definition there can be three types of spastic cerebral palsy. *Hemiplegia* is when either the right or the left side of the body is affected by spasticity; other parts of the body remain unaffected. *Diplegia* is when the legs are affected; the arms are usually unaffected or only slightly so. *Quadriplegia* is when all four limbs are affected.
- **Athetoid cerebral palsy** is when children have difficulty in maintaining a position and make involuntary movements. Since the movements are hard to control, it may take a great deal of effort to achieve a desired action or activity. Speech can be affected, owing to abnormal movements of the oral musculature and vocal cords.
- **Ataxic cerebral palsy** is the least common form of cerebral palsy. The child has unsteadiness of movement and poor balance, walking may be jerky, hands can be shaky, speech development may be slow and spatial awareness may be impaired.

Causes

Cerebral palsy can be caused by an injury to the brain, before, during or after birth. It can be caused by:

- a difficult or premature birth;
- bleeding in the baby's brain;
- an infection caught by the mother during pregnancy.

Treatment

Cerebral palsy cannot be cured. It is non-progressive in that the level of brain damage does not get worse. Pupils with cerebral palsy will have a physical management programme devised by a physiotherapist/occupational therapist to maximise a pupil's functional abilities. Some pupils may have orthopaedic surgery to release tendons thus improving the range of movement. Others may have botulinum therapy to relax and lengthen specific muscles. Selective dorsal rhizotomy is also considered.

> **For further information contact:**
>
> Scope
> www.scope.org.uk
>
> Further details can also be found in the book in this series entitled *Supporting Children with Cerebral Palsy*.

Educational implications

Not all pupils with cerebral palsy will have learning difficulties. Depending on the part of the brain that has sustained an injury, pupils may experience varying degrees of difficulty in some or all of the following areas:

- mobility;
- co-ordination;
- fine motor skills;
- concentration;
- attention and listening skills;
- visual perception;
- speech and language;
- speed of processing receptive language;
- vision;
- hearing;
- eating and drinking skills;
- dressing;
- toileting.

It is important that an inter-disciplinary approach is adopted when assessing and planning to meet the needs of pupils with cerebral palsy. Strategies are included in later sections of this book. The following points should be taken into consideration:

- restricted mobility necessitating use of a wheelchair or mobility aids;
- difficulty climbing stairs or accessing the first floor in a wheelchair;
- difficulty sitting on the floor during carpet time and assembly;
- PE lessons may require differentiation;
- a physical management routine may need to be incorporated in the school day – when and where will it be implemented?
- time for liaison with outside agencies and funding to release staff for training in the use of specialised equipment;
- manipulation of standard classroom equipment. Is specialised equipment or a compensatory approach required? ICT equipment should be considered;
- positioning of equipment to aid independent access;
- organisation of personal effects such as the school bag;
- disabled toilet access with support arrangements to assist with personal care issues, this may include hoisting;
- arrangements for out-of-school visits with home/school transport if required.

10 Club foot (talipes) and limb-lengthening treatment

Definition

There are four known kinds of club foot. The most common is called 'talipes equinus-varus', which describes the heel as being drawn up and turned inwards. Sometimes the condition just affects one foot and at other times, both.

Cause

The condition is more prevalent in boys than girls and although the medical profession has been aware of it for many years, its actual cause is unknown. There is evidence that this condition runs in families and is hereditary.

The position in the womb may determine the type of condition present and there is some suggestion that there are links with a reduced amount of amniotic fluid or 'oligohydramnios'.

Treatment

The condition can be detected prior to birth by ultrasound. However, it is not usually discovered until after the child is born. Although this condition causes stress and anxiety to parents, it is usually treatable with a great deal of success and the child can make equally good physical progress as those children without the condition.

The treatments used in this condition vary with the severity. The baby's foot is manipulated into position and then put into a cast, which is repeated weekly for about five weeks. This is followed by a quick procedure on the tendon to allow a greater range of movement. Special splints/boots will then be worn for a long period of time – during the day then just at night. It is possible also to use casting rather than strapping. Relapse is possible as children grow and in some more severe cases, surgery will be used. Surgery will involve the lengthening of affected tendons and ligaments and then the limb is put in plaster.

The surgical treatment for talipes is sometimes the same as, or similar to, limb-lengthening surgery. Here, the bones are broken and re-set with a growth space, using an external fixator (metal cage).

For further information contact:

www.clubfoot.co.uk

Educational implications

Advice is usually available from the orthopaedic department or the physiotherapy department involved in the treatment of pupils with this condition. Pupils who have had limb-lengthening surgery or talipes surgery may return to school with an external fixator (metal cage). The family will have received instruction on how to care for the pin sites and how to turn the screws to facilitate gradual lengthening. Schools should not be required to adjust the screws on an external fixator or to care for pin sites. Pupils generally need to have their leg elevated on an extended support attached to a wheelchair.

The following points may need to be taken into consideration when planning for a pupil to return to school following limb-lengthening surgery:

- physical access to the school building and positioning of the classroom on the ground floor;
- access to a toilet sufficiently spacious to accommodate a wheelchair with a leg extension;
- position within the classroom for ease of entry and exit;
- height of tables, to accommodate the extended leg;
- supervision during non-teaching time, e.g. breaks and lunchtimes;
- alternative activities for PE lessons;
- planned absences to attend hospital on a regular basis, which may require 'catch up time';
- where and when physical management routines, recommended by the physiotherapist to prevent muscle wastage during the treatment period, can be implemented;
- if home/school transport is required: LA to be contacted, if necessary.

11 Cystic fibrosis

Definition

Cystic fibrosis (CF) is the most common, life-threatening, inherited disease, affecting over 10,000 white people in the UK. It is a rare condition in other ethnic groups.

Causes

Cystic fibrosis is caused by an abnormal gene on chromosome number seven which controls the movement of salt and water in and out of the cell. Diagnosis usually takes place in early childhood because chest infections and chronic gastro-intestinal malabsorption cause a 'failure to thrive'. A 'sweat test' can detect an abnormal amount of chloride ions. Diagnosis is then confirmed by genetic tests, which can detect one of the recognised CF genes.

Symptoms

The lungs and digestive sytem become clogged with mucus, making it hard to breathe and digest food. The symptoms can be:

- a persistent cough;
- excessive saliva and mucus;
- shortness of breath;
- recurrent chest infections;
- recurrent fatty diarrhoea if correct treatment is not received;
- constipation;
- blockage of the bowel resulting in severe pain;
- poor absorption of nutrients leading to poor growth.

Further symptoms may include sinusitis, enlarged liver and spleen, diabetes and fertility problems.

Treatment

- There is no known cure for cystic fibrosis although research is progressing into gene therapy.
- Life expectancy is reduced but the prognosis is improving as treatment develops.
- Regular physiotherapy is needed to clear harmful mucus from the lungs.
- Frequent courses of antibiotics are used to treat recurrent chest infections, taken orally, inhaled through nebulisers or intravenously.

- Pancreas defects are treated by enzyme supplements (in capsule form), which assist the digestion of protein and fat. These are taken with meals.
- Other symptoms are treated as necessary.
- Exercise is important as it helps clear mucus and improves physical strength.
- A suitable diet is important, i.e. one which is high in energy, as a pupil with it has to work harder, and rich in fat and protein to compensate for that lost in stools.

For further information contact:

Cystic Fibrosis Trust
enquiries@cftrust.org.uk
www.cysticfibrosis.org.uk

Educational implications

There is no evidence to suggest that pupils with cystic fibrosis have learning difficulties. However, they can be late in reaching developmental milestones due to their early failure to thrive. Academic progress can sometimes be affected by frequent and sometimes prolonged absences from school as a result of chest infections or hospitalisation.

As with other medical conditions, schools should work with other agencies, including medical professionals, to ensure the needs of the pupil are met in the mainstream setting. Most of the physical management routines such as chest physiotherapy are carried out at home. Extra physiotherapy may be required in school when the pupil has a chest infection (training will be given by the physiotherapist).

There are a number of issues which should be considered when planning to meet the needs of a pupil with cystic fibrosis.

- Access to a small private room when extra physiotherapy or nebuliser treatment is required, should be available.
- Supervision should be provided at lunchtime, for younger children who are not yet able to manage their own medication.
- Be aware that pupils with CF may be embarrassed about their persistent cough, small stature and having to take tablets with all food.
- Full participation in PE lessons is generally recommended because it helps to loosen sputum in the lungs. Be aware that the pupil with CF may feel unusually tired and lethargic following a chest infection.
- Arrangements to minimise infection, such as being allowed to stay inside at breaks during cold damp weather, should be considered.
- Older pupils may have portable intravenous antibiotic equipment. PE and boisterous play may not be recommended if this equipment is in use.
- Examination concessions may need to include:
  - additional time up to 25%;
  - administration of treatment during a supervised break;
  - arrangements to take examinations outside school, e.g. hospital/home;
  - treatment can be given during a supervised break;
  - the Joint Council for the GCSE (Standing agreement no 4) should be consulted.

- A record of health-related absences should be kept as evidence for the examination boards.
- Pupils may need to catch up on work missed.
- Ensure social interaction when a pupil has frequent absences from school.
- It should be ensured that pupils eat their lunch, which will need to be high in calories.
- Normal rebellious adolescent behaviour can have serious consequences for the teenager with CF. Faddy diets and neglected physiotherapy are common issues.
- Older pupils may be in denial of the potential seriousness of the condition. This is a coping mechanism; sympathetic understanding and counselling may be needed. Caution is advised when offering counselling. Pastoral staff should check with parents about how much knowledge the pupil has about his or her condition and how much the parents want them to have.
- Delayed onset of puberty may cause anxiety: boys are likely to be infertile although not impotent, and girls can have serious health problems if they become pregnant. Special sex counselling may be required.
- The psychological pressures arising from the chronic nature of the condition will affect the whole family.
- Pupils with CF should not meet in person another person with CF because of cross-infection.
- Careers advisers may wish to contact the Cystic Fibrosis Trust Support Service for advice relating to career and job prospects. Pupils with CF can cope with most jobs except those that are physically demanding or environmentally unsuitable.

12 Diabetes

Definition

Diabetes Mellitus is a common condition which occurs when the amount of glucose in the blood is too high and cannot be used properly by the body.

Glucose comes from sweet sugary foods and starchy foods such as potatoes and bread. Some meats such as liver also produce these sugars. Insulin, made by the pancreas, helps to provide energy for the body. Insulin would normally control the amount of sugar in the blood; levels of insulin fall during activity.

There are two types of diabetes. Type 1 develops when the body is unable to produce insulin; it is known as insulin-dependent diabetes and usually occurs before the age of forty. Type 2 is when the body produces insufficient insulin; it is known as non-insulin-dependent diabetes and usually occurs after the age of forty. Around 33,600 children and young people have Type 1 diabetes.

Causes

The condition occurs when the pancreatic cells that produce the insulin are destroyed. The actual cause is not known, it is thought to be triggered by some viruses.

Symptoms of diabetes are generally:

- extreme thirst;
- excessive passing of urine;
- extreme fatigue;
- blurred or affected vision;
- thrush.

The condition does develop fairly quickly, more in weeks than months, and symptoms are very evident.

Treatment

Treatment for diabetes tries to maintain glucose levels and blood pressure level as near to normal as possible. It also aims to protect against long-term damage to the eyes, kidneys, nerves, heart and major arteries. Diabetes is usually treated by insulin injections, regular physical activity and attention to diet. Sometimes those with the condition need other medication/tablets.

Educational implications

The pupil with diabetes will require an Individual Health Care Plan.

- Every member of staff should be aware of the pupil's condition, understand the Individual Health Care Plan (IHCP) and know what to do in an emergency.
- Training to meet the pupil's medical needs should be delivered to all staff involved from the appropriate health professional.
- Pupils will need to monitor their blood glucose levels when at school. It should be decided in conjunction with the pupil where this is carried out, i.e. in the classroom or away from it. A blood glucose check involves pricking the finger and putting a drop of blood onto a test strip, which then goes into a meter.
- Tests will be needed before meals, before, during and after physical activities, if pupils are unwell or if staff feel levels are wrong (this should be part of the IHCP).
- Schools should consider where the blood glucose checking kit, insulin and snacks will be stored.
- It should be easily accessible, wherever the pupil is, e.g. on the school playing field, on an off-site visit.
- Younger pupils will require support to administer tests but older pupils should be able to administer tests themselves. Pupils with SEN will need help.
- Pupils may need to inject insulin during the school day. An appropriate place should be assigned (the toilet area is not suitable). Safe disposal of materials should be available.
- Pupils with diabetes should have access to drinks of water when they require them.
- Pupils may need to visit the toilet more frequently. It should be accepted that the pupil be allowed to go when necessary, without seeking permission. A discreet system should be in place, e.g. placing a token on the teacher's desk to ensure they are aware of the pupil's absence from the room.
- Pupils will require a snack at break time or in lesson time as a part of their medical care. (It is the family's responsibility to provide this.) Staff should check to ensure the snack has been taken.
- Pupils should participate in PE lessons. However, this can lower glucose levels. They may need to take an extra snack before or after participating and levels checked. Check if pumps need disconnecting before contact sports.
- Pupils should be able to participate in off-site school trips. A planning meeting will be necessary with parents, particularly if an overnight stay is involved. Risk assessments should take place. Ensure all equipment, medication and snacks used at home are readily available throughout the residential visit. Emergency contact numbers should be taken, the IHCP which addresses the pupil's needs must be carried. Further information can be obtained by contacting the pupil's named diabetes specialist nurse. Activity, different food, changes in routine, stress and excitement can all affect blood glucose levels.
- Pupils may need a meal plan. Parents should ensure that the school is notified of dietary needs. A paediatric dietician will contact schools if there are any special

dietary requirements. When possible, pupils with diabetes should be allowed to go in the first sitting at lunch time.

- Plans may need to be in place for catching up on work if lessons are missed.
- Adjustments will need to be made for examinations, including:
  - all staff being aware of the pupil's condition;
  - testing of glucose levels during the exam;
  - drinks and snacks available;
  - supervised toilet breaks;
  - sitting close to an adult in case a hyper/hypo occurs;
  - extra time in case of the above;
  - plans for the above should be in the IHCP.

A 'Type 1 diabetes at school' pack can be ordered from Diabetes UK.

13 First aid/emergency responses

The following give some indicators of the signs and symptoms in a pupil with diabetes, which require a response:

Hypoglycaemia (low glucose levels)
Signs:
- mood changes;
- loss of concentration;
- feeling shaky;
- headache;
- dizziness;
- sweating;
- pale appearance;
- glazed eyes.

Hyperglycaemia (high glucose levels)
Signs:
- unresponsive;
- unconscious.

Severe hyperglycaemia is a medical emergency.

School staff should be aware of the signs and symptoms, which requires treatment, all of which should be detailed within the Individual Health Care Plan (IHCP). All staff should be aware of what constitutes the need for intervention and what is an emergency situation. Designated staff with appropriate training should respond according to the IHCP. This will have been devised in conjunction with the appropriate health care professionals and parents.

14 Eczema

Definition

Eczema describes a group of skin conditions, affecting all ages. Those affecting children include atopic eczema, allergic contact dermatitis, irritant contact dermatitis and infantile seborrhoeic dermatitis.

It is thought that 20% of school-aged children have eczema and one in twelve adults continue to be affected.

The severity of eczema can vary from mild cases where the skin is hot and itchy, to severe cases where the skin is broken, raw and bleeding.

Cause

The causes can be very varied. Atopic eczema is thought to be hereditary. It is also believed that people with atopic eczema are sensitive to allergens in the environment. In these cases the child often has asthma and hay fever. Other types of eczema can be caused by irritants such as chemicals and detergents.

Treatment

- Minimising environmental allergens can help.
- External medications such as cortisone cream and moisturisers.
- Itching can be relieved by antihistamines.
- Secondary infections may require antibiotic treatment.
- Cortisone can be given in pill or injection form, when other medications fail.

For further information contact:

National Eczema Society
Hill House
Highgate Hill
London N19 5NA
Tel: 0870 241 3604 (Eczema Information Service)
www.eczema.org

Educational implications

Skin conditions, such as eczema, can cause severe discomfort and distress for some pupils. Eczema is sometimes exacerbated by stress. This leads to frantic itching, resulting in damage and bleeding to the affected areas.

The following advice relates to general issues for consideration when planning the management of this condition in schools. Any proposed changes to the current care regime must be fully discussed with the parents and included within an Individual Health Care Plan. Help in drawing up a health care plan may be sought from the school nurse and the parents.

- Pupils should be encouraged to participate in all activities.
- They should be encouraged to develop the ability to identify occasions/activities when their skin will need extra attention.
- Careful monitoring of skin reactions to specific activities is necessary. Close liaison with parents is advised.
- Some pupils benefit from the use of emollient creams as a barrier or preventive measure, to be used before playing with sand, water, paints, clay and other potential irritants.
- Ask parents for a small pot of emollient to allow pupils to top up after wet play or hand washing.
- Most pupils with eczema cannot tolerate synthetic fibres. Use of 100% cotton clothing is often recommended wherever possible. This may have implications for dressing-up activities.
- Flexibility with uniform may be required, e.g. tight ties may irritate.
- Synthetic cotton wool may cause irritation for some pupils. Note: cotton wool is frequently used in Christmas decorations and similar materials are used for stuffing toys.
- Soap is an irritant for many pupils, ask parents for an alternative.
- A personal 'towel' may be required.
- Pupils should be kept on task to minimise opportunities for scratching, as this can lead to bleeding sores if unchecked. Concentration can be affected. Ask parents for their distraction techniques.
- Consideration should be given to the pupil's position in the classroom if he/she reacts to sunlight and excessive dust.
- The classroom should be well ventilated and pupils should be encouraged to remove layers of top clothing if the classroom is warm.
- Pupils may find that their pencil grip is affected if their hands are badly affected by the eczema. A fat pencil or a pencil grip can help. Use of ICT may be more comfortable.
- Chlorinated water causes problems for many pupils. Barrier cream may be required before swimming. Showering and application of cream is likely to be required afterwards.
- Increased irritation at night can cause a lack of sleep, which impacts on the pupil's ability to access education the next day.

15   Epilepsy

Definition

Electrical activity happens all the time in the brain. A seizure occurs when there is a sudden burst of intense electrical activity in the brain. This causes a temporary disruption to the way the brain normally works, making the brain's messages mix up. Seizures are a symptom of the condition, and the type of seizure experienced indicates the area of the brain affected.

- Epilepsy affects 600,000 of the UK population.
- In 70% of cases it can be controlled by medication.
- Most of those with childhood epilepsy will grow out of it.

Causes

Whether an individual develops epilepsy depends on two factors: their inherited threshold level (primary epilepsy) and life circumstances (secondary epilepsy). Any of the causes below would come under the heading of 'life circumstances':

- brain damage due to a difficult birth;
- a severe blow to the head;
- a stroke which starves the brain of oxygen;
- blood chemical abnormalities, e.g. low calcium, magnesium or glucose;
- an infection of the brain, such as meningitis;
- very rarely, a brain tumour.

Seizures fall into two groups – either generalised seizures occurring across the whole brain, or partial seizures affecting one area only.

Types of seizures

- **Childhood absence seizures** (previously known as 'petit mal'), which are the most common form of childhood epilepsy.
- **Tonic-clonic** (previously known as 'grand mal'). This is the classic seizure of which most people are aware in which the pupil loses consciousness.
- **Benign Rolandic seizures** (previously known as 'simple partial seizures'), which are confined to one area of the brain and consciousness may or may not be lost.
- **Complex partial seizures** during which the pupil either loses consciousness completely or becomes vague, looks dazed and does not respond when spoken to.

- **Atonic drop attacks** (rare) during which there is a sudden loss of muscle tone and the pupil falls to the ground.
- **Myoclonic seizures** (also rare) – a sudden contraction of the muscles which causes a jerk. It can affect the whole body but often only one or both arms.
- **'Status epilepticus'** is when a seizure lasts for more than the usual length of time (approximately 5–10 minutes) or if the pupil has recurrent seizures one after another. Follow the emergency procedure which forms part of the pupil's Individual Health Care Plan.

Possible triggers of seizures

- Forgotten or incorrect medication.
- Illness/high temperature.
- Lack of sleep or food.
- Emotional stress.
- Excitement/boredom.
- Flashing lights (very rare, 3–5% only).
- Changes in hormone levels.
- Drugs/alcohol.

Long-term treatment

Effective seizure control is gained in 70% of those with epilepsy by use of the correct medication. Also:

- avoidance of all known seizure 'triggers' helps;
- brain surgery (very rare).

For further information contact:

Epilepsy Action
Tel: 0808 800 5050
www.epilepsy.org.uk

National Society for Epilepsy
Tel: 01494 601437
epilepsysociety.org.uk

Young Epilepsy
Tel: 01342 832243
www.youngepilepsy.org.uk

Educational implications

Epilepsy affects about 60,000 young people under the age of 18.

Every school should therefore be familiar with the condition of epilepsy and plan to meet the individual needs of each pupil. The headteacher and governing body need to:

- ensure an Individual Health Care Plan is in place;
- develop a 'Whole School Policy' to meet the needs of pupils with epilepsy;
- raise awareness of the condition amongst staff through INSET and ensure that all staff are familiar with the management of Tonic-Clonic seizures in school;
- ensure all staff including dinner supervisors etc. are aware of the pupil's needs;
- nominate staff to administer drugs – N.B. this must be on a voluntary basis;
- arrange for the training of nominated staff;
- identify an easily accessible area for storage and administration of drugs;
- keep accurate records of seizures occurring and pass on to parents;
- monitor changes in mood, behaviour, learning;
- share relevant information with staff bearing in mind issues of confidentiality;
- identify 'at risk' factors (e.g. triggers of seizures) for an individual pupil.

General school organisational issues

Anti-epileptic medication gives 70% of pupils the opportunity to lead normal lives. However, the following are considerations which apply to the remaining 30% of pupils.

- Ensure that new staff are made aware of the school policy.
- Timetable lessons on the ground floor if possible, for safety reasons.
- Certain subjects, namely science, food technology, PE and some elements of art, will involve safety issues.
- Assess the need for adult supervision during movement between classes or break times.
- Encourage peer support and empathy through circle time (in agreement with parent and pupil). Young Epilepsy has resources to educate.
- Encourage the development of a whole-life ethos to reduce the incidence and consequences of seizures, e.g. learning to pace themselves etc.
- Include pupils in school outings and residential visits, ensuring adequate supervision and careful planning.
- Likewise, pupils should participate in sports wherever possible following advice regarding safety.
- Be aware of the emotional aspects on the pupil, e.g. fear of having a seizure, embarrassment.
- Ensure good communication with the pupil's family.

Specific advice

Tiredness and lethargy

- Encourage parents to pass on information regarding nocturnal seizures (home/ school book).

- Note the problem and possible learning missed and keep records to pass on to consultant/parents.
- Provide differentiated work if appropriate.

Photosensitivity

- For the 3–5% of those who fall into this group, care will need to be taken when using computers, e.g. fit a glare screen if necessary, take regular breaks away from the screen (Health & Safety Guidelines).
- Sit the pupil in the shade in a sunny classroom.
- Ensure they wear sunglasses outside during the summer.

Teaching implications of epilepsy

Be aware that:

- the type, frequency and duration of seizure;
- the original cause (i.e. brain damage) and area of the brain involved;
- poor self-image, social factors and side effects from medication

may impact on:

- learning;
- concentration;
- memory;
- behaviour;
- language and communication skills;
- fine and gross motor skills;
- self-esteem.

Careers

- Specific advice will be required – Young Epilepsy may help.

16   Haemophilia

Definition and cause

Haemophilia is a group of blood disorders in which there is a defect in the blood clotting mechanism. Haemophilia is a lifelong, inherited genetic condition affecting people from all races, and mainly boys. The clotting factors in normal blood are numbered from I to XIII. There are two main types of haemophilia, A and B, with haemophilia A accounting for most cases. Both have the same symptoms but are caused by different clotting factors and have slightly different treatments. The symptoms are internal bleeding, usually around joints and muscles, causing pain and stiffness:

Treatment

- *On demand* treatment is used in response to an episode of prolonged bleeding.
- *Preventative treatment* is used to prevent episodes of bleeding and subsequent joint and muscle damage. Regular injections of clotting factor medication are given, often by parents and later by the pupil. An implantable port is sometimes used to administer the treatment.
- Regular monitoring appointments will be required.

> ### *For further information contact:*
>
> Haemophilia Society
> Tel: 0207 939 0780
> www.haemophilia.org.uk

Educational implications

Pupils with haemophilia bruise easily. However, it is a misconception that they bleed excessively from normal cuts and grazes. Spontaneous internal bleeding into the joints, muscles and other parts of the body can occur. Pupils generally recognise the 'feel' of internal bleeding before external signs such as bruising and swelling are visible. It is therefore essential that staff listen to a pupil if he reports these 'feelings'. Several points should be considered prior to admitting a pupil to school. A health care plan should be written ensuring that the following are included:

1. what constitutes an emergency for this pupil;
2. what procedures should be followed if a pupil feels a 'bleed';
3. emergency contacts in case parents/guardians are unavailable.

The Individual Health Care Plan should be drawn up in consultation with the parents and a medical practitioner such as the haemophilia support nurse.

- Health and Safety policy regarding handling bodily fluids. There should be clear guidelines regarding handling of bodily fluids, provision of hygiene requisites such as gloves, and disposal and cleaning routines. DfE advice suggests all bodily fluids should be handled as though there were a possibility of HIV transmission.
- Awareness raising – relevant staff, volunteers and pupils should be aware of the guidelines for dealing with spillage of blood (and other bodily fluid).
- Confidentiality – the pupil's full medical history should not be disclosed without permission, to protect his or her privacy under the Human Rights Act. Issues such as Hepatitis, HIV and AIDS can cause undue prejudice and/or hysteria in a school community. If these conditions are disclosed by a pupil, parent or health care worker they should be dealt with in strict confidence and with sensitivity.
- Mobility support may be required following 'bleeds' which result in swelling or pain.
- Planning for out-of-school activities would include all the above points.
- Additional support or alternative activities in PE lessons may be required. Sporting activities can be categorised as low/medium or high risk according to level of exertion, need for protective gear and potential for contact with other pupils.

Low/medium risk	Medium risk	High risk
Swimming	Rounders	Football at senior level
Dancing	Cricket	Rugby at senior level
Sailing	Baseball	Hockey
Athletics, cycling	Motor cross/motor cycle	Judo at training level
Skiing		Wrestling, boxing
Soccer, baseball		
Racquet sports		

Seek professional guidance from a medical professional who supports the pupil.

First aid procedures

Remember:

- wear gloves for any open bleeding;
- clean up blood spills using 10% bleach solution and paper towels – dispose of in a strong plastic bag, via the clinical waste disposal service or by incineration.

Cuts and abrasions

Small cuts, scrapes and bruises do not usually cause problems. Cover with a plaster or dressing, apply pressure. Deep cuts that need stitching will require treatment at the haemophilia centre.

Mouth and tongue bleeds

These can be hard to control because blood clots are washed away by saliva or by food. Try giving the pupil an ice cube or an ice lolly to suck. Treatment at the haemophilia centre will be required if the bleeding does not stop.

Joint bleeds

Main signs of internal bleeding are pain or a 'funny feeling', swelling, warmth of the skin at the site of the internal bleed, loss of movement in the joint or muscle. Younger pupils may not recognise these signs: watch for the pupil protecting a joint by limping or not using it and treat as soon as possible at the haemophilia centre.

Face, neck and throat injuries

These must be treated promptly by parents or the haemophilia centre.

Head injury

a) **Bumps to the head** – if the pupil is not distressed or in pain, the bump is not likely to have caused any problems. If in doubt send for treatment. As with all head injuries, *inform parents so that the pupil can be observed for 12 hours.*

b) **Minor head injuries** – bumps that lead to bruising and small cuts should always be treated either by the parents or the haemophilia centre. As with all head injuries, *inform parents so that the pupil can be observed for 12 hours.*

c) **Serious injuries** – if the pupil receives a heavy blow to the head or is unconscious, an ambulance should be called.

Symptoms which would indicate the need for medical intervention:

- persistent or increasing headaches;
- vomiting;
- sleepiness or a change in behaviour;
- weakness/clumsiness in arm/leg;
- stiffness or pain in the pupil's neck;
- blurred/double vision, crossed eyes;
- poor balance;
- fits or convulsions.

The above is general information; the pupil should have an Individual Health Care Plan giving detailed guidance relevant to their condition.

17 Head injury, accidents, meningitis, brain tumour, stroke

Definition

A head injury is any kind of injury to the head and/or the brain. The brain is a dense mass of nerve tissue. It rests on the base of the skull, surrounded and bathed by cerebrospinal fluid.

Injury, either by accident, infection, stroke, or brain tumour, might result in loss of function in one or more areas of the brain due to damaged or torn nerve tissue and/or blood vessels.

Causes

Accidents, including road traffic accidents (RTAs)

- In any accident the extent of the injury depends on the severity and type of accident, e.g. fall, impact, or blow to the head.
- Road traffic accidents are the most common cause of severe head injury in children.
- In these cases impact to the head results in injury, both at the site of the blow and to the area directly opposite, as the brain rebounds off the inside of the skull (similar to injury resulting from shaking).
- Initial damage might range from:
  - superficial bruising or cuts;
  - skull fracture;
  - subdural haematoma (a blood clot between the skull and the surface of the brain) at the site of the blow;
  - to possible loss of consciousness.
- Complications may follow owing to bruising and swelling of the brain, causing increased pressure within the skull. Pressure is put on blood vessels, cutting off oxygen to the nerve cells, and on the brain stem (at the base of the brain) which regulates breathing, heart beat etc.
- If an object penetrates the skull and brain, there might be consequent neurological infections.
- Depending on the area of the brain injured, paralysis, impaired vision or memory, and possibly onset of epilepsy may be short-term, or long-term, consequences. Post-traumatic loss of memory is also common.

Meningitis

- This condition is the result of viral or bacterial infection causing inflammation of the meninges, the membranes which cover the surface of the brain and spinal cord.
- Eighty per cent of cases are seen in children under 15 years of age and most of these occur in the under-fives.
- The most serious form is bacterial meningitis. Types include pneumococcal, streptococcal, and the most common haemophilus influenza type B. This is the cause of meningitis in the 1–4 year age range.

Recognising meningitis

- Symptoms of *viral meningitis* include headache (worse on bending), fever, nausea and vomiting, dislike of bright lights, and a stiff neck. In more severe cases there might be muscle weakness, paralysis, impaired speech or double vision.
- Symptoms of *bacterial meningitis* include any of the above, but also a rash of red spots, drowsiness and eventual coma.
- If meningitis is suspected, call for medical assistance as quickly as possible.
- Hospital treatment is usually a lumbar puncture (to test cerebrospinal fluid). If meningitis is confirmed, massive doses of antibiotics are given, together with fluids to prevent dehydration. It might also be necessary to use a ventilator to aid breathing, due to pressure on the brain stem.
- Vaccinations help prevent the spread of infection.

Brain tumour

- Cells die and are replaced constantly. Occasionally the blueprint for a cell will go wrong and the 'wrong' pattern reproduces itself again and again causing a 'tumour'. These can be either benign (non-cancerous) or malignant (cancerous).
- Possible treatment of a malignant tumour might be surgical removal, chemotherapy, or radiotherapy that is carefully targeted to kill the cells.
- Benign tumours are usually surgically removed.
- Epilepsy is a common consequence of a brain tumour, owing to the invasive nature of such growths.

Stroke

- A stroke is the result of a blood clot blocking a small artery or blood vessel. This cuts off oxygen to that area of the brain, killing nerve cells. Additional damage may be caused by brain swelling.
- Hospital treatment consists of medication to reduce brain swelling and the possible use of a ventilator to assist breathing if pressure is put on the brain stem.
- The resulting difficulties depend on the area in which the stroke occurred and the extent of the damage to nerve cells.
- The most common symptoms of stroke are paralysis or numbness down one side of the body, dizziness and loss of balance, speech difficulties and visual impairment.
- These can be long or short term depending on how quickly treatment was begun and the recuperative abilities of the brain.

- Although rare, very young children may have a stroke. Recuperation is generally better than for adults with good long-term prognosis.

Treatment of head injury following an accident in school

- If the injury occurs in school, follow the normal first aid procedure and seek medical advice if necessary.
- Be aware that a lack of external injury to the head does not always indicate the extent of damage to the brain.
- Always monitor the pupil for any after effects, particularly concussion (i.e. tiredness or nausea), difficulties with swallowing or coughing for no reason. Seek medical advice as soon as possible.
- For more serious accidents, resulting in loss of consciousness, bleeding from the ear or a seizure, do not move the pupil unless he/she is at further risk of injury.
- Call the emergency services immediately and inform parents.

Hospital treatment

At the hospital, medical treatment may include skull X-rays and/or a brain scan, medication to reduce swelling, or surgery to remove blood clots.

Occasionally, pressure on the brain stem causes breathing difficulties and a ventilator is needed to aid breathing.

For further information contact:

Headway Brain Injury Association
www.headway.org.uk

HIRE (Head Injury Re-Education)
Tel: 0115 941 0006

Meningitis now
www.meningitis.org

The Brain Tumour Charity
www.braintumourcharity.org

The Stroke Association
www.stroke.org.uk

Educational implications

By the time a pupil who has sustained a head injury is ready to return to school, he/she will be in the recovery phase, which may or may not last for many months. It is difficult to generalise advice for pupils returning to school following a head injury, as the degree of difficulty can vary enormously according to the age of the pupil and the area and extent of damage.

The difficulties experienced by those pupils whose injuries have resulted in severe physical disabilities are likely to be obvious, in that they are visible. For example:

- mobility problems;
- paralysis or loss of function in a limb.

Other difficulties may not be so easy to detect, but may also have a significant impact on the pupil's ability to access the curriculum. For example:

- visual impairment;
- epilepsy;
- reduced stamina;
- speech or hearing difficulties;
- short- and long-term memory problems;
- emotional and behavioural problems.

It is essential that schools be given as much information as possible about the pupil's condition, prior to his/her return, so that appropriate strategies can be put in place.

Refer to Sections IV–VI for possible strategies to deal with the following issues:

- accessing the building;
- accessing the curriculum;
- alternative recording strategies;
- supporting short-term memory problems;
- developing organisational skills;
- developing concentration skills/promoting listening skills;
- developing visual perception;
- developing self-esteem;
- promoting positive peer group relationships;
- emotional issues.

18 Heart conditions

Definition

This is the term given to abnormalities of the heart present from birth. They affect approximately one in every 133 babies born in the UK.

Cause

It is sometimes difficult to determine the cause of the problem. Children's heart conditions usually develop during pregnancy; in some cases the problems may be genetic. The underlying problem, however, whatever the cause, is the abnormal development of the heart.

Listed below are the most common types of heart condition affecting children:

- *Aortic Stenosis* describes how the aortic valve, situated between the aorta and left ventricle, is very narrow, meaning that flow of blood from the left ventricle into the aorta is less efficient.
- *Atrial Septal Defect* describes a hole between the left and right atrium; there are often no symptoms in childhood and there may be gradual damage to the heart muscle.
- *Pulmonary Atresia* is a blockage between the right ventricle and the pulmonary artery.
- *Coarctation of the Aorta* describes part of the aorta as being very narrow, thus impeding the flow of blood to other areas in the body. Babies usually require surgery. In older children symptoms can include tiredness, cramps, heart murmur, and high blood pressure in the arms and a weak pulse in the legs.

Heart murmurs

Although a heart murmur is not a particular illness, it indicates that there is some irregularity in the passage of deoxygenated blood, which should return via the veins to the heart. The word 'murmur' describes a 'swishing' sound in the blood. Heart murmurs may not be detected until the child is about 2 or 3 years old, as the child has to be calm and quiet for the detection of this condition, which is difficult to hear.

Overweight and heart disease risk

The problems connected with overweight include high cholesterol, diabetes and especially heart disease. This in turn causes breathlessness, movement difficulties and the possibility of more serious repercussions. In consultation with the GP, it is possible to recommend safe diets for overweight children. An exercise regime may also be recommended to manage weight problems. This must be at all times in consultation with the child's doctor.

Treatment

Treatment of heart conditions can include surgery or a series of operations which will either improve function or correct the abnormality.

For further information contact:

British Heart Foundation
www.bhf.org.uk

Contact A Family
209–211 City Road
London EC1V 1JW
Tel: 020 7608 8700
Helpline: 0808 808 3555
www.caf.org.uk

Children's Heart Federation
Helpline: 0808 808 5000
www.chfed.org.uk

Educational implications

Many older pupils with congenital heart conditions are able to be self-limiting within school and therefore manage their condition independently. Generally, cognitive ability is not affected by the heart condition. However, staff should be aware that lack of concentration could be associated with a decrease in arterial oxygen, which is most likely to occur after physical exertion.

There are some pupils who require a variety of support arrangements according to their individual need. These may include:

- young pupils may need quieter activities and monitoring to guide to these;
- placement of tutor group, room allocation, timetabling issues, with reference to frequency of climbing stairs;
- additional adult support to monitor the child's condition, e.g. becoming bluish;
- assistance with movement around school and transportation of belongings;
- provision of an additional set of textbooks to minimise the volume of books to be carried to and from school;
- storage facilities for personal belongings to reduce the weight of the school bag;
- additional support in design and technology and practical science lessons, to minimise physical demands of the lesson: masks may be required in D&T to prevent inhalation of dust; in addition, the pupil may have to avoid science experiments that involve fumes and/or smoke;
- alternative activities during PE lessons, or opportunities to take rest breaks during a lesson;

- suitable furniture (e.g. perching stools) to take account of the effect of prolonged standing in practical lessons;
- a stair climber or lift may be required to allow access to upstairs classrooms;
- a wheelchair that is compatible with the stair climber may be required for mobility around school when necessary;
- a small trolley to use in the dining room, or a buddy to carry a tray;
- access to home tuition may be required following surgery, or during prolonged periods of absence;
- encourage peer interaction during long absences and on return to school;
- accurate sharing of information about the pupil's condition to all staff;
- reducing the timetable and giving time for 'catch up';
- flexibility by staff regarding the timescale for completion of homework, due to fatigue;
- arrangements to allow the pupil to maintain fluid intake during or between lessons, without asking permission, if this is required;
- opportunities to have healthy snacks if necessary, to maintain energy levels;
- a particular diet may be required and advice from medical staff should be followed;
- arrangements for the pupil to remain inside at breaks and lunchtimes during inclement weather and avoid outdoor activities;
- establishment of appropriate monitoring and liaison strategies with continuity of additional adult support to enable careful monitoring of the pupil's condition and regular liaison with parents, if necessary;
- careful positioning within the classroom, as the pupil may need to avoid sitting in direct sunlight. Classrooms should be well ventilated;
- awareness of the need for the pupil to be as independent as possible;
- administration of medication according to the Individual Health Care Plan (see 'Managing medicines on school premises', pages 95–7);
- a need to be aware of the side effects of medication, e.g. diuretics will mean more trips to the toilet;
- anticoagulants will mean pupils should take care not to get bruised so rough playground games and contact sports must be avoided.

19 Hip problems

Definition

Developmental dysplasia of the hip (DDH) describes a variety of conditions in which the ball and socket of the hip do not develop properly. In the mildest forms, the socket may fail to grow deeply enough. In the more severe forms, the femoral head or ball may be displaced completely out of the socket and be dislocated.

Causes

Although there are no definite causes of hip problems such as DDH, there are a number of factors that may be relevant to the disorder:

- breech birth or breech position in the last three months of pregnancy;
- a family history of hip problems or double jointedness;
- lack of fluid surrounding the baby in the womb (oligohydramnios);
- the increase in maternal hormones before delivery may make the susceptible baby's hip more likely to displace at the time of birth;
- wrapping a baby's legs too tightly after birth;
- girls are more often affected than boys, particularly the first born;
- hip problems are more common in babies who have mild foot deformities or tightness in the neck.

Treatment

If the condition is detected around the time of birth, a lightweight splint which holds the legs apart (abducted) may be applied. The splint is worn for several weeks and is only removed at the clinic. Some children do not respond to early treatment while others are not detected until they are older. The approach to treatment for this group is slightly different, and a number of treatment options are available:

- admission to hospital for X-rays and a short period of traction;
- a small operation in the groin area under a general anaesthetic;
- use of a 'broomstick' cast;
- a more extensive operation to put the ball and socket in place.

It is normal to put the child in a plaster of Paris/fibre glass cast known as a hip spica. Treatment in plaster will continue for several weeks or months and may be followed by a period in a splint. After a short stay in hospital most children return home with visits to the Outpatient Clinic for check-ups. Some children may return to school in a hip spica.

The prognosis is generally good when diagnosed early and treated accordingly, although normal mobility may be delayed. There is also a tendency towards arthritis later on, with additional complications such as irritable skin or slight inequalities of leg length.

For further information contact:

http://steps-charity.org.uk/hip problems

Educational implications

Advice is usually available from the orthopaedic department or the physiotherapy department involved in the care of pupils with these conditions. The majority of children are diagnosed in infancy and with successful treatment will not present with difficulties in school. A few pupils, however, may have residual pain and/or limited mobility, following late diagnosis, treatment and during the rehabilitation period.

The following are general considerations:
- Symptoms of joint pain and stiffness can vary from day to day.
- Rest is recommended for severe pain, some pupils require analgesia (pain killers) in school. Rest is best done at home if pain is severe.
- Risk assessments, advice from health professionals may be needed before the pupil returns to school.
- Restricted mobility may, in some cases, require use of a wheelchair over long distances. It is not usually necessary for pupils to stay in their wheelchairs within the classroom. This may have an impact on out-of-school visits and school transport arrangements. Risk assessments should be carried out.
- Additional support may be required.
- Adaptations and/or extra equipment, e.g. a specialist table to go over a wheelchair may make the pupil more comfortable.
- Pupils may have difficulty sitting on the floor during carpet time and assemblies.
- Prolonged sitting in examinations can contribute to discomfort. Additional rest breaks can be requested through the examinations officer.
- Low-impact exercise, walking, swimming, cycling, is very good for pupils with these conditions. High-impact sports and contact sports should be avoided.
- Pupils can generally be relied upon to be self-limiting in physical activities.
- Long absences from school are possible following orthopaedic surgery. In a minority of cases home tuition may be recommended.
- In rare instances, pupils may need to return to school whilst in hip spica or broom-stick plasters. In these instances additional support may be required for toileting, mobility and transport issues. Local Authority funding may be requested.
- Close liaison between the family, health professionals and other relevant outside agencies will ensure changing needs can be met.

20   Hirschsprung's disease

Definition

Hirschsprung's disease is a serious childhood condition, which occurs once in 5,000 births. It is a genetic disorder, which results in a lack of spontaneous bowel movements, which can lead to chronic constipation and/or diarrhoea, vomiting, lack of appetite and abdominal distension.

Cause

Children born with this condition have a section of bowel which is permanently squeezed and narrow. Stools become stuck and form a blockage.

Treatment

It is usual for the affected portion of bowel to be surgically removed and the healthy sections rejoined. A single procedure known as a 'pull through' operation is frequently performed. This is where the affected portion of the bowel is removed and the healthy bowel is joined to the rectal wall. Sometimes a colostomy is required prior to this operation if the child is too small or too ill. The colostomy operation involves bringing the colon out to the surface of the abdomen through a surgically formed hole called a stoma, so that the stools can be discharged into a special pouch for disposal.

Most children have no long-term complications after successful surgery to repair the bowel. However, there is a significant minority of children who continue to experience constipation, encopresis (stool incontinence) or persistent enterocolitis (inflammation of the large and small intestine).

Educational implications

Some pupils who have Hirschsprung's disease are likely to have periods of bowel incontinence during their time at school. For some pupils the emphasis, therefore, must be placed on independent management of their bowel incontinence rather than toilet training. It is likely that a pupil with Hirschsprung's disease will experience leakage of fluid matter rather than solid faeces. Some pupils will be oblivious to, or will deny the existence of the odour, whereas other pupils will be highly sensitive to the possibility that classmates will detect an odour.

Consider the following points:

- sensitive sharing of information regarding the condition, with relevant staff;
- access to a private toilet facility with waste disposal and washing facilities;
- arrangements to enable the pupil to leave the classroom discreetly when necessary;
- arrangements to ensure a supply of clean underwear and wet wipes are available;
- access to drinks, as a regular fluid intake is usually recommended.

Self-management in early years (see Section II for detailed strategies)

The emphasis should be placed on establishing a routine where the pupil checks his/her nappy/trainer pants/underwear for signs of soiling at regular intervals, with adult support. Additional visits to the toilet will be required to deal with soiling incidents identified by smell.

Self-management in Key Stage 1 (see Section II for detailed strategies)

Building on the work done in Early Years, the pupil will be encouraged to initiate visits to the toilet at regular intervals. He/she should be encouraged to take responsibility for as much of the cleansing and changing routine as is possible.

Self-management in Key Stage 2 (see Section II for detailed strategies)

The pupil should now be encouraged to implement his/her cleansing and changing routine independently with oversight for emotional support and guidance. It is hoped that independence will have been achieved well before secondary school transfer.

Self-management in Key Stages 3 and 4 (see Section II for detailed strategies)

Pupils generally manage their own cleansing and changing routines at KS3/4. It is essential that staff are sensitive to the pupil's need for privacy. Some pupils have difficulties around the time of puberty and can begin to deny that they have a problem. This may result in peer pressure.

Colostomy bag

- If a colostomy bag or ileostomy bag is in place, staff training from a health care professional will be required.
- A room to carry out procedures will be necessary with disposal equipment available.
- An intimate care plan should be in place.

21 Hydrocephalus

Definition

Hydrocephalus is a build-up of fluid on the brain. The excess fluid puts pressure on the brain and can damage it.

If the drainage pathways are blocked at any point, the fluid accumulates in the ventricles inside the brain, causing them to swell. In babies and infants, the head will enlarge. In older children and adults, the head size cannot increase as the bones which form the skull are completely joined together.

Two types affecting children

Congenital hydrocephalus

Present at birth and caused by birth defects, e.g. spina bifida or an infection in the mother during pregnancy e.g. rubella, and carries the risk of long-term mental and physical disability.

Acquired hydrocephalus

May occur after a serious head injury or a complication of a medical condition, e.g. a brain tumour.

Treatment

Some forms of hydrocephalus do not need any treatment. Some types of hydrocephalus require surgery. This usually involves inserting a shunting device to drain the excess cerebro-spinal fluid, thus preventing a deterioration of the condition. The shunt does not cure the condition; it does, however, control it. The symptoms which were caused by raised pressure do normally improve; however, other problems can still remain.

> *For further information contact:*
>
> Shine
> www.shinecharity.org.uk
>
> ASBAH
> www.mencap.org.uk

Educational implications

Not all pupils with hydrocephalus will have learning difficulties: ability levels range from severe learning difficulties to above average ability. It is therefore important that staff do not have preconceived ideas about an individual pupil's ability. Pupils of average ability who have hydrocephalus may appear to have more problems than their peers in:

- focusing on their work;
- thinking and working independently;
- assessing the standard of their own work.

In addition some pupils with hydrocephalus may have the following.

Poor short-term memory

- struggles to remember instructions;
- has difficulty taking part in class discussions and listening to stories;
- has difficulty remembering facts, e.g. addition facts and multiplication tables;
- has problems acquiring reading and spelling skills.

Short attention span

- is easily distracted by external stimuli.

Faulty spatial awareness and visual perceptual deficits

- has difficulty in judging distances – bumps into furniture, walls, misses targets;
- has a poor sense of direction.

Spatial and perceptual difficulties are most frequently observed in the following areas:

PE

- off-the-floor activities;
- field activities;
- target activities.

Presentation skills

- setting out work/writing on lines;
- drawing and completing tables/charts;
- copying from the board.

Maths

- may find algebra difficult because of problems recognising patterns;
- will find spatial relationships and symmetry difficult;
- will have difficulty sorting objects.

Practical lessons

- may find difficulty handling tools safely, e.g. cutting along a line, judging distances between containers when pouring fluids.

Lack of motivation and initiation

- may sit and wait for individual instructions rather than follow class instructions;
- needs verbal prompts to start work;
- may have difficulty participating in class discussions.

Inability to generalise

- has difficulty taking concepts learned in one area and applying them to another;
- may require frequent and deliberate over-learning;
- may not realise that a reprimand has been given to a group of pupils.

Difficulty understanding inference, takes everything very literally

- for example, a teacher might say to the class, 'Wake up!' … the pupil with hydro-cephalus might respond, 'I'm not asleep.'

Sequencing difficulties/poor organisational skills

- appears to be poorly organised in thought and action (links with memory problems).

Poor concept of time

- no inclination to hurry;
- five minutes can seem the same as an hour.

Poor hand function

- many pupils with hydrocephalus have weak hand skills;
- many pupils find neat handwriting impossible to achieve.

Classroom observations and teacher assessment will identify strengths and weaknesses and will inform the individual education plan (IEP). Pupils may require educational targets and or physical targets. Sections IV and V may provide suggestions for these.

Health care considerations for pupils with hydrocephalus

Many pupils with hydrocephalus have a shunt fitted. Blockage of a shunt will result in raised pressure within the brain and can have serious consequences if undetected. School staff need to be aware that the following symptoms could indicate a problem:

- sudden or recurring headaches;
- vomiting;
- seizures;
- raised temperature;
- unusual listlessness and apathy;
- change or deterioration in vision.

An Individual Health Care Plan is required to outline the medical condition, state what constitutes an emergency for this pupil and what procedures need to be followed.

22 Hypermobility syndromes

Hypermobility describes over-flexibility of the joints. Hypermobility syndromes refer to a family of conditions which have over-flexible joints in common, although the cause and degree of involvement may be different. Additionally individual members of a family may be affected to a greater or lesser degree. It is more common in females.

All the conditions involve problems with the supporting tissues of the body, i.e. ligaments, tendons, joints and muscle, due to faulty proteins in the connective tissue that would normally act as 'glue' and give the body its strength. Individuals with these conditions inherit looser and more fragile connective tissue. People with hypermobility are particularly supple and able to move their limbs into positions others find impossible. There can be difficulties:

- pain and stiffness in joints and muscles;
- fatigue;
- dislocation of joints;
- recurrent injuries, e.g. sprains;
- digestive problems;
- dizziness;
- stretchy skin.

It is estimated that 7–10% of children have loose joints and occasional pain ('growing pains'). Most grow out of it as joints become stronger.

Benign joint hypermobility syndrome (BJHS)

This lies at the mild end of the hypermobility continuum and is autosomal dominant, i.e. 50% of the offspring will carry the gene for the condition. The abnormal protein for this condition is collagen Type 1 (the most common). Some individuals show little evidence of joint problems.

Ehlers-Danlos syndrome (EDS)

Ehlers-Danlos syndrome is made up of a large group of conditions that has now been reduced to six major subtypes, which are classified and diagnosed by their individual symptoms. Ehlers-Danlos Hypermobile Type (formerly EDS III) and BJHS are now considered to be the same condition. EDS is inherited in a variety of ways, mostly by a dominant gene from either parent, while other forms may require a recessive gene from both parents. Occasionally it is linked to the X chromosome, which causes the condition in boys. 'Types' tend to run true for each family.

Prevalence is between 1 in 5,000 and 1 in 10,000.

In addition to having hypermobile joints, individuals with EDS also have differences in skin texture. Joint problems range:

- from hyperextensible joints (i.e. they move beyond the normal range of movement);
- to lax joints which are liable to dislocate.

Skin fragility might show itself in:

- soft and velvety skin;
- more elastic skin which tears or bruises easily;
- slow and poor healing of wounds;
- development of pseudotumours (fleshy lesions over scar or pressure areas).

Less common problems associated with some types of EDS are arterial/intestine/uterine fragility, scoliosis, mitral valve prolapse and gum disease.

Diagnosis is based on family history and clinical findings.

Treatment

- By teaching joint protection through careful management of physical activities.
- Sometimes joints may require splinting to improve support, e.g. the ankles.
- Skin care is again by teaching self-management to protect skin, e.g. using sun block or covering up during sunny weather.

Marfan syndrome

This lies at the more severe end of the continuum. In this condition the disorder of the connective tissue is the result of a genetic defect affecting the body's production of fibrillin, a protein that is the main component of microfibrils. These allow tissues to stretch repeatedly without weakening. Mostly the condition runs in families, inherited by an autosomal dominant gene, although in 25% of cases it results from a spontaneous mutation on chromosome 15.

Prevalence is between 1 in 3,000 and 1 in 5,000 of the population.

Individuals are typically tall and thin with disproportionately long arms and legs, fingers and toes. The disorder affects three systems of the body:

- bones and muscles;
- the heart and circulatory system;
- the eyes.

Bones are longer than usual, and ligaments weaker, therefore greater stress is placed on joints. Problems may be experienced in the following areas:

- the spine, e.g. scoliosis (sideways curves), kyphosis (outward curve) etc;
- inward curving sternum resulting in breathing difficulties;

- possible flat feet and/or frequent pain in the feet;
- hip problems.

Problems with the circulatory system result from the walls of blood vessels/heart being weaker and stretching more than usual. In particular the individual may have:

- aortic enlargement;
- aortic regurgitation (blood leaking back into the heart);
- a 'floppy' mitral valve (the valve between the chambers of the heart).

Eye problems range from myopia (short sight), dislocation of the lens, glaucoma or retinal detachment. Lungs can also be affected resulting in pneumothorax (collapse of a lung) and other chest conditions.

Diagnosis is based on family history and clinical findings.

Treatment

- Treatment is based on individual needs. Children are regularly checked for scoliosis of the spine; given an electrocardiogram (ECG) to check for heart problems, and eye checks.
- Pain in the feet can be treated with medication and sometimes individuals wear inserts in their shoes to support the feet.

Beals Syndrome (Beals arachnodactyly syndrome)

This is a rare genetic connective tissue disorder which is autosomal dominant. Individuals have:

- long, thin 'spider-like' fingers and toes with congenital contractures of the fingers, hips, elbows, knees and ankles;
- scoliosis/kyphosis of the spine;
- crumpled ears;
- possible mitral valve prolapse.

Treatment is by surgery (to lengthen tendons), splints to support major joints (e.g. ankles and feet, wrists etc.) and input from the physical and occupational therapists to build muscle strength and develop self-help (dressing, eating and toileting) strategies.

For further information contact:

Contact a Family (CaF)
Helpline: 0808 808 3555
www.cafamily.org.uk

Ehlers-Danlos Syndrome
www.ehlers-danlos.org

Nord (National Organisation of Rare Disorders)
www.rarediseases.org

Hypermobility Syndrome Association
www.hypermobility.org

Marfan Association
www.marfan-association.org.uk

Educational implications

The majority of pupils with these syndromes will require an Individual Health Care Plan to indicate areas of concern and strategies to overcome them. It would also help to look at the book in this series, *Supporting Children with Co-ordination Difficulties* since these pupils experience similar problems with low muscle tone. Whether a pupil has a statement or Education, Health and Care (EHC) plan will depend on the extent of his/her physical needs.

If there is a greater physical need, pupils will be under the oversight of a physiotherapist and possibly an occupational therapist for joint care and to develop life skills. Often a physical management programme will be sent to the school and the therapist will visit on an arranged basis to review progress. Additional areas for consideration are as follows.

Access

Many pupils will have problems with access and may have difficulty:

- using stairs (use ramps or lifts instead);
- opening heavy doors or those with automatic closers; adjust pressure to make it easier for pupils to open, or fit electro-magnetic door stops;
- negotiating a busy classroom, e.g. trip hazards.

Stamina

Stamina falls off dramatically as the day progresses. Staff should ensure that:

- parents send in high-energy, slow-release snacks, e.g. bananas, raisins, grain bars etc. for play breaks and ensure that the pupil has plenty of fluids;
- the pupil's wheelchair/buggy (if used) is sent in prior to outings/visits and if necessary a pre-visit has been made to look at wheelchair access;
- allow extra time for written work;
- consider the use of ICT.

Gross motor management/PE

Staff will need to ensure that the pupil does not:

- take part in rough and tumble play/activities (depending on the severity of the condition);
- participate in contact games/sports;
- put undue pressure on joints, e.g. running/jumping;
- over-exercise thereby causing damage to joints.

Fine motor skills

- Pupils will usually have problems with fine motor activities owing to low muscle tone.
- Consider the appropriate pencils, use of ICT.

Skin care

- Consider the need for sun block on sunny days until the pupil is able to self monitor.
- If bruising occurs, use ice pack to reduce swelling and inform parents.

23 Juvenile arthritis

Definition

Juvenile arthritis (JA) is also known as juvenile rheumatoid arthritis and juvenile idiopathic arthritis. It is a condition which begins before the age of 16 and causes inflammation in one or more joints, stiffness, swelling, pain and loss of motion. The number of children known to have JA is 1 in 15,000. Juvenile arthritis may be difficult to diagnose because some children may not complain and joint swelling may not be immediately obvious. Limping, a reluctance to walk or a reluctance to use both hands may represent early signs. The condition can follow different patterns, which may require different treatments.

There are different kinds including:

Oligoarthritis is the most common type and mostly affects the knees. It is mild and may go but may develop inflammation of the eye.

Oligoarticular JA is the most common form of childhood arthritis. It affects four or fewer joints with symptoms being swollen and painful joints, especially the knees and/ or ankles. There can also be eye problems.

Polyarticular JA affects more than five joints and causes pain and stiffness in joints and tiredness and eye inflammation.

Mobility will be affected and difficulties with handwriting and manipulating equipment may be experienced.

JA is a fluctuating condition so the pupil may function better on some days than others, some pupils may have stiff joints in the morning which improve as the day passes.

Causes

The precise cause of JA is as yet unknown. It is not thought to be directly inherited and it is rare for more than one family member to be affected.

Treatment

- Painkillers, disease-modifying anti-rheumatic drugs.
- Anti-inflammatory drugs can used to ease the condition.
- Eye drops may be necessary.

- Physiotherapy and occupational therapy helps to reduce pain, increase joint function and prevent joint contractures.
- An exercise plan.
- Joint protection.

For further information contact:

Arthritis Research UK
www.arthritis.researchuk.org

Educational implications

Pupils with arthritis are usually under the care of a rheumatology consultant, who may recommend the involvement of a range of health professionals. Physiotherapy input would maintain joint mobility; occupational therapy advice may be given regarding daily living skills; an ophthalmologist may screen children with arthritis for iritis (a particular type of irritation); a podiatrist to provide foot orthoses. The following issues may need to be considered when planning to meet the educational needs of a pupil with arthritis:

- empowerment/independence – how the pupil will be enabled to be independent and make his/her own decisions;
- the fluctuating nature of the condition will result in good days and bad days;
- energy levels/motivation – a pupil who experiences constant or frequent pain can be debilitated and have depleted energy levels. Some pupils 'switch off';
- mobility – the pupil may be ambulant for some of the time and need a wheel-chair or buggy for the rest. In more severe cases, a powered wheelchair may be required;
- fine motor adjustments – handwriting may be affected during flare-ups, consider the use of ICT;
- furniture – a chair of an appropriate height and a tilting writing surface may be required, to prevent back and neck hunching;
- give support in subjects such as Design Technology to use equipment;
- home tuition/catch-up strategies – frequent absences may be unavoidable;
- social/academic isolation can be the result of frequent absences, peer support through emails, text messages, letters and cards can help;
- home/school transport should be provided, if required;
- physical management routines – when, where, by whom;
- compliance – consider how to react if the pupil refuses to co-operate with physical management routines;
- self-care skills – restricted movement in joints may cause difficulty with personal hygiene routines. Where can the pupil receive discreet support?
- eyesight – be aware that redness of the eyes can be an early sign of iritis. Monitor and mention to parents;
- restricted growth management implications (see section on restricted growth).
- joint protection issues will require further advice from the occupational therapist;
- medication may be required in school.

24 ME (myalgic encephalomyelitis) or CFS (chronic fatigue syndrome)

Definition

The correct term, chronic fatigue syndrome (CFS), or myalgic encephalomyelitis (or encephalopathy) (ME) is debated:

- ME or myalgic encephalomyelitis is felt to reflect that fatigue is the only symptom;
- CFS or chronic fatigue syndrome is a serious condition that can cause long-term illness and disability but may improve over time. It is most used because there is little evidence of brain and spinal inflammation as the term ME implies.

Children between 13 and 15 can be affected.

Cause

The cause has not been completely identified. It could be:

- a viral infection;
- immune system problems;
- hormone imbalance;
- stress or trauma.

Common symptoms

Symptoms range from mild to severe:

- painful muscles;
- digestive difficulties;
- constantly feeling unwell;
- sore throat;
- all common flu-like symptoms;
- overwhelming fatigue of mind and body;
- poor concentration and short-term memory difficulties;
- sleeping disorder;
- painful lymph nodes;
- fluctuating temperature;
- depression, panic attacks;
- intolerance to light, sound, certain foods.

Some effects

- Disrupted education/employment.
- Restricted social life.
- Those most severely affected may be housebound or bedridden.

Treatment

This can vary and aims to reduce symptoms, including:

- cognitive behaviour therapy;
- a structured exercise programme;
- medication to control pain, nausea and sleeping difficulties.

The recovery rate is both variable and unpredictable. It may be either short- or long-term. Sometimes recovery is only partial, with remissions and relapses. However, it is not generally thought to be a degenerative condition.

For further information contact:

The ME Association
4 Corrigan Road
Stanford-le-Hope
Essex SS17 0AH
Tel: 01375 642466
www.meassociation.org.uk

www.afme.org.uk

Educational implications

Pupils who have been diagnosed with ME or CFS are usually absent from school for a prolonged period, during the acute period of their illness. This is usually followed by a planned re-introduction to the school day. During the rehabilitation period, pupils have to learn how to live within their energy levels and carefully pace their activities, balancing physical and mental activity and rest.

- The pace of re-introduction is generally recommended by the consultant and supervised by the GP and/or the school doctor.
- Pupils who are severely affected will need home tuition until they are sufficiently recovered to begin a phased return to school.
- Some pupils may only be able to attend on a part-time basis.
- Others may continue at school with reduced activity particularly in PE and games.
- Assistance may be required with getting around the site, particularly in large secondary schools.
- Use of ICT may be easier than using pens and pencils.
- Support peer group interaction by encouraging peers to contact the pupil through social media (with parental approval).
- Home/school transport may be required.

25   Muscular dystrophy

There are a number of different types of muscular dystrophy which share three common features: they are hereditary, progressive and each follows a characteristic pattern. The term 'dystrophy' refers to a progressive weakness of the muscles due to a breakdown of the muscle fibre. At present there is no known cure for this group of conditions. Medical and surgical management along with physiotherapy and occupational therapy can improve the quality of life for children with these conditions.

The common forms of muscular dystrophy affecting children are:

- Duchenne muscular dystrophy;
- Becker muscular dystrophy;
- Congenital myotonic dystrophy;
- Emery-Dreifuss muscular dystrophy;
- Facioscapulohumeral muscular dystrophy;
- Myotonic dystrophy;
- Spinal muscular atrophy.

Duchenne muscular dystrophy

This form of muscular dystrophy mostly affects boys. The condition may be diagnosed between the age of one and three when the child is unable to walk, run and jump like other children of his age. The child might struggle to get up from the floor and have difficulty climbing the stairs. Sometimes a diagnosis is not made until after the child starts school.

Between the ages of eight and eleven most boys become unable to walk. They can develop scoliosis of the spine. By mid-teens they may have heart problems (dilated cardiomyopathy). It is likely that by their late teens or twenties respiratory muscle weakness will make breathing harder; the heart may also be affected. Life expectancy will be shortened.

Becker muscular dystrophy

Becker muscular dystrophy is a milder form of dystrophy affecting males and developing later in childhood. Becker dystrophy progresses at a much slower rate. Symptoms may be noticed in childhood. These could include muscle cramps and poor performance in sports at school. Loss of mobility does not usually occur until adulthood.

Congenital myotonic dystrophy

Congenital myotonic dystrophy is present at birth; the baby is very weak and has difficulty breathing, sucking and swallowing. Motor and speech development is delayed. There may be learning difficulties; however, there can be deterioration in late childhood and early adolescence. Some children with this type of dystrophy will start school using a wheelchair.

Emery-Dreifuss muscular dystrophy

This develops in childhood or early adulthood. It initially causes muscle contractures in the arms, neck and feet.

Facioscapulohumeral muscular dystrophy

This affects males and females, although males earlier and more severely. Some do not become aware of symptoms until adulthood. Teenagers may have shoulder aches, rounded shoulders and face, upper arms and back and calves will become affected.

Myotonic dystrophy

Myotonic dystrophy can develop at any age. Life expectancy is not always affected unless it is a severe form. It is progressive muscle weakness and muscle wasting. The muscles to be affected are the face, neck, hands, forearms and feet first. It can also result in muscle stiffness, cataracts, sleepiness, swallowing problems, learning and behaviour difficulties.

Spinal muscular atrophy (SMA)

There are several different types of SMA affecting children with differing onset ages and of differing severity. It can affect both boys and girls. It is due to deterioration in the nerve cells connecting the brain and spinal cord to the body's muscles.

Type I (severe) – present at birth or shortly after birth. Children generally do not survive beyond the second year.

Type II (intermediate) – symptoms usually occur in babies from 7–18 months old. People can live long lives.

Type III (mild) – onset usually about 18 months. The child will be able to walk and will have a normal lifespan.

Treatment

There is no cure for MD but the folllowing will be put in place:

- Mobility – physiotherapy, low-impact exercise, physical aids.
- Breathing assistance – machines to assist breathing, particularly at night.
- Steroid treatment improves muscle strength and slows down weakening for six months to two years.
- Swallowing difficulties may necessitate altered consistency of food, possible surgery or feeding through a gastrostomy tube.
- Corrective surgery to improve posture.

Educational implications

It is important that pupils with the muscular dystrophy group of conditions are given experiences that add to their quality of life. Education provides opportunities for pupils with muscular dystrophy to have the same expectations and experiences as other pupils. It is important that pupils are prepared for adult life in the same way as their peers, regardless of the prognosis of their condition.

Planning for changing needs

Key stages have been used as a very general guide to the possible timescale for the progression of Duchenne muscular dystrophy. The prognosis for youngsters with Duchenne muscular dystrophy is now changing owing to the development of steroid treatment, which can in some cases extend mobility into the early teens, and ventilatory support, which can possibly increase life expectancy into their twenties. Life expectancy is increasing with drug intervention.

Note: Other dystrophy conditions may progress at a slower pace. Some pupils may start school using a wheelchair.

Key Stage 1

- Some pupils may start school before a diagnosis has been made.
- Parents may need a great deal of emotional support. This in turn can create a need for emotional support for staff who work closely with the pupil.

- Staff may request information about the condition and how it is likely to progress. Be aware that parents are unlikely to be able to pass on this type of general information. The Family Care Officer, who is employed by the Muscular Dystrophy Society and is based at the regional centre, could be contacted via the physiotherapist for staff INSET.
- Outside agencies gradually become involved. The physiotherapist is likely to be a regular visitor, providing training and monitoring of a physical management routine.
- Designation of space for a physical management routine should be implemented.
- Identification of special educational needs should flag up future needs for the Education Health Care (EHC) Plan with the LA/educational psychologist/parents.

The following are difficulties which may be experienced by the pupil:

- If the pupil struggles to get up from the floor, encourage him/her to use the furniture to push up on. Discourage him from using the heads of other pupils for balancing when getting up from sitting in a group. Provide a chair as an alternative to sitting on the floor when transferring to standing from sitting becomes difficult. The physiotherapist and occupational therapist will monitor changes of position and advise on suitable seating.
- The pupil may have increasingly frequent falls in the playground, but adult oversight should be non-intrusive. The physiotherapist will advise on the level of adult intervention.
- Supervision when moving around the school is advisable. If support is unavailable, position the pupil near the teacher and adjust the pace of movement accordingly.
- Handrails may be required in the toilets next to urinals and in the cubicle to aid balance. They may also be needed next to external doors that have steps.
- If PE activities become demanding, provide activities that offer degrees of difficulty. Seek advice from the physiotherapist.
- Stamina levels can be affected, consider timetabling of strenuous activities such as PE or climbing the stairs to the ICT suite to the morning when the pupil is more likely to be fresh.
- Stamina can change as the week progresses. By Friday, the child may be falling more frequently but stamina may be improved after the weekend break. Fatigue related to late nights could have a physical consequence.
- Physical performance can also be affected by minor ailments such as colds.
- Handwriting might become tiring. Introduce keyboard skills early so that the skill has been established before there is a need.
- Pupils may experience difficulties with reading, spelling and language throughout the key stages.
- Self-image can be affected. Some pupils become very passive and avoid making decisions. Staff should consider their own attitudes and approaches to ensure that the pupil with muscular dystrophy is allowed to be independent and to make his/her own decisions.

Key Stage 2 (all of the above KS1 issues plus)

- An EHC is likely to be in place to provide additional adult support.
- Timetable in downstairs classrooms.
- The pupil may become progressively weaker and walking becomes restricted.

A wheelchair is usually used by the end of Key Stage 2. A powered chair may boost the pupil's self-esteem.

- The physiotherapist is likely to introduce specialist equipment such as a standing frame and a wheelchair into the daily management routine. Standing frames can be timetabled for use in art and design and technology when other pupils are usually standing.
- Assistance will be needed when transferring between classroom chairs and wheelchairs. Support staff are required to attend a Moving and Handling training course.
- A timetable will help to plan where equipment is best used and physiotherapy sessions will take place.
- Oversight is generally required in the playground.
- Provide alternative activities for PE lessons.
- Assistance is required to collect meals, possibly to cut up food. The occupational therapist may recommend lightweight cutlery.
- Access to a disabled toilet facility is required when the pupil is no longer able to use a standard toilet independently. Specialist equipment such as a hoist and commode chair may be required.
- Some pupils present challenging behaviour as their physical ability deteriorates.
- The emotional implications for staff working closely with pupils with Duchenne muscular dystrophy should be considered and support offered as necessary.

Key Stages 3 and 4 (all of the above KS1 and 2 issues plus)

- Most pupils with Duchenne muscular dystrophy are 'off their feet' by the time they begin secondary school. All moving and handling procedures will be carried out using a hoist and sling. This will be recommended at the appropriate time by the physiotherapist; a multi-disciplinary assessment is likely to be instigated to recommend moving and handling procedures.
- Mobility difficulties have implications for access to specialist teaching rooms in schools with several floors. Access to upper floors is possible with a stair climber to carry the pupil in a manual wheelchair or through use of the lift.
- Hand skills become weaker; therefore, a lightweight word processor will be useful for recording written work. Keyboard skills should have been established in KS1 and 2.
- A compact keyboard may become necessary as the student's range of arm movement becomes limited.
- Stamina becomes a more significant issue. The support assistant may have to act as a scribe for longer pieces of work.
- Additional adult support is required for all physical tasks.
- The physical management programme becomes more complex as the condition progresses. Curriculum access is often compromised. A restricted curriculum may be necessary. Consult the Educational Psychologist.
- Students may be offered spinal surgery during their time in secondary school. This would have implications related to absence. Liaison with the relevant Hospital Tuition Service may be required.
- Careful planning for work experience placements is required.
- Promote good peer relationships.
- Post-16 provision planned with the expectation of future employment being a realistic goal.

26 Perthes disease

Definition

Perthes disease is a condition in which the head of the femur flattens due to temporary lack of a sufficient supply of blood to the area. Perthes disease is most common in boys between the ages of 3 and 12 and can run in families. It most commonly affects one hip although both hips can sometimes be affected.

Causes of Perthes

There is a flattening of the top of the femur, when the supply of blood to the area is insufficient, causing the surface of the bone to deteriorate. Eventually the blood supply returns and the femoral head heals (usually within two years). There may be a resulting deformity of the femoral head which causes hip problems. The following symptoms may occur when Perthes disease is suspected:

- limited mobility;
- hip movement impeded by stiffness;
- shortening of leg;
- constant pain in the thigh;
- problems with walking, often limping;
- painful knee;
- wasting of upper thigh muscles.

Treatment of Perthes

Treatment for this condition varies, some children will need treatment. Some children will attend regular hydrotherapy to help stop the hip from stiffening, to ease pain, to help build up muscles and to hopefully regain the range of movement in their hips. Regular X-rays will take place. Simple traction: bed rest for 7–14 days. Pain relief is given. Surgery may be necessary to improve the function or position of the hip.

This condition usually runs its course within two to four years.

Educational implications

Advice is usually available from the orthopaedic department or the physiotherapy department involved in the management of pupils with Perthes disease. Many pupils have residual pain and/or limited mobility, throughout the rehabilitation period.

The following are general considerations:

- Symptoms of joint pain and stiffness can vary from day to day.
- Rest is recommended for severe pain; some pupils require analgesia (pain killers) in school. Rest is best done at home if pain is severe.
- Restricted mobility may, in some cases, require use of a wheelchair over long distances. It is not usually necessary for pupils to stay in their wheelchairs within the classroom. This may have an impact on out-of-school visits and school transport arrangements.
- Pupils may have difficulty sitting on the floor during carpet time and assemblies.
- Prolonged sitting in examinations can contribute to discomfort. Additional rest breaks can be requested through the examinations officer.
- Low-impact exercise – walking, swimming, cycling – is very good for pupils with these conditions. High-impact sports and contact sports should be avoided.
- Pupils can generally be relied upon to be self-limiting in physical activities.
- Long absences from school are possible following orthopaedic surgery. In a minority of cases home tuition may be recommended.
- Close liaison between the family, health professionals and other relevant outside agencies will ensure changing needs can be met.

27 Prader-Willi syndrome

Definition

The incidence is approximately 1:15,000 births and it occurs in both males and females. It is a chromosomal condition. Pupils may exhibit any of the following characteristics:

- **hyperphagia** (excessive appetite) caused by a failure in the mechanism which tells a person that they have had sufficient food. Babies with PWS show little interest in feeding but between the ages of one and four interest in food increases and it can become an insatiable obsession. Some children can control food intake but others eat at every opportunity whether it be appropriate or not, e.g. taking other people's food, eating food from bins. Unless the diet is carefully controlled, weight gain can be very rapid and considerable problems result;
- **hypotonia** (low muscle tone) possibly resulting in speech problems, poor fine motor skills, poor gross motor skills and delayed toileting;
- **short stature** which results in height which is below average;
- **hypogonadism** causes delayed or arrested puberty;
- **temperature control** can be poor and there can be a risk of overheating or hypothermia;
- **high pain** threshold which can mask symptoms of illness and safety risks, e.g. danger from hot water;
- **eyesight problems** as a result of myopia (short-sightedness), strabismus (abnormal alignment of the two eyes) and nystagmus (involuntary movement of the eyes causing reduced depth perception, poor eye–hand co-ordination);
- **curvature of the spine** during the growing period;
- **dental or oral problems** – thick or sticky saliva resulting in 'crusting' at the corners of the mouth, a poor quality of tooth enamel and a small jaw resulting in overcrowding of the teeth;
- **speech and language delay** – expressive language is generally being more impaired than receptive language;
- **cognitive ability** varies from moderate to severe learning difficulty to a learning ability within the average range;
- **behavioural characteristics** which can include temper outbursts, resistance to change, obsessive and/or compulsive behaviour, possessiveness of items to which they are attached, stubbornness;
- **immature social skills** may be restricted and need to be taught; relationships with adults are usually good;
- **sleep problems** as breathing may be interrupted during sleep, which is worsened by weight gain;

- **perseveration** can occur (i.e. persistent talking or questioning about a topic);
- **skin picking** can become obsessive and, owing to high pain thresholds, the pupil may not feel any discomfort – an increase in this activity can be related to stress;
- **friendly, sociable, kind and caring with a good sense of humour.**

Causes

Prader-Willi syndrome (PWS) can be caused by more than one genetic abnormality; in 70% of cases the genetic abnormality is called a deletion, i.e. a piece of chromosome 15 inherited from the father is missing. In 20–30% of cases PWS occurs when two chromosome 15s are inherited from the mother and none from the father. It is thought that this results in a malfunction of the hypothalamus (an area of the brain), which is responsible for causing the symptoms of PWS.

Treatment

- Hormone treatment to address growth issues.
- Advice will be given from a wide range of health professionals, e.g. paediatricians, dieticians, physiotherapists, occupational therapists, speech and language therapists and professionals in education.

For further information contact:

www.pwsausa.org

Educational implications

There are a number of issues which may need to be taken into consideration when supporting a pupil with PWS.

Diet

Diet has to be carefully monitored (calorie intake should be lower than that of other children), which has implications for portions given for school meals, food which is permissible at snack time and school parties. It may be helpful if the whole class group eats in a healthy manner in order to support their peer with PWS. Tuck shops, cafeteria-style catering and food technology lessons may also cause difficulties. Advice should be taken from parents. Supervision is needed as pupils may eat anything, whether it is suitable or not; stealing food is not unknown. Storage of lunchboxes should be away from the classroom.

Fine motor skills

Fine motor skills should be developed from the earliest stages. Alternative recording strategies and support to manipulate equipment may be required.

Gross motor skills

The younger pupil may require support to develop independent movement around school. Exercise is important: older pupils may need encouragement to take part in

PE lessons and care should be taken when teams are being chosen so as not to leave the pupil with PWS until last.

Short stature

Consideration may need to be given in order to achieve access to equipment.

Delayed puberty

Sensitivity may be required when sex education lessons are given. Privacy may need to be given to teenage boys when changing for PE as physical development may be different from their peers.

Temperature regulation

Pupils with PWS may be either too hot or too cold and may need oversight and encouragement to wear the appropriate clothes for the weather.

Memory problems

The short-term memory required for remembering instructions may be limited, strategies to support this may be required. Consolidation and revision of skills and information learned will be necessary.

Poor vision related to Nystagmus, Strabismus and Myopia

Pupils may need longer to see objects, take longer to read print (which may necessitate longer time for examinations) and require larger print. They may need to be placed appropriately in the classroom to see the teacher and read information from the white board.

Daytime sleeping

Pupils may fall asleep during lessons. They should be encouraged to stay awake by moving to different activities of a short duration. If sleep is unavoidable help will be needed to catch up on information missed.

Delayed toilet training

Schools may need to implement a toilet training programme in conjunction with parents.

Behaviour problems

Routines are important: being aware of the signs of a temper tantrum and diffusing or distracting from the situation may help, together with a quiet area to calm down. Behaviour management strategies may be required.

Skin picking

An increase in this habit can be a sign of stress, so the pupil should be observed for causes. Praise should be given when skin is not picked.

Problems with saliva

The pupil should be encouraged to drink quantities of water.

High thresholds of pain

Be aware that the pupil with PWS has a high pain threshold. Check for injury after falls and monitor closely in potentially hazardous activities in lessons such as Design Technology.

28 Restricted growth (including achondroplasia)

Definition

Restricted growth may be the result of over one hundred medical conditions. They can be divided into two main categories: proportionate and disproportionate short stature.

Proportionate short stature (PSS)

Growth is restricted throughout the whole body and may be associated with chronic heart, lung, kidney or liver disease. In Turner's syndrome restricted growth may be the only symptom prior to puberty; however, learning difficulties are a common feature. Other growth disorders include Silver Russell syndrome, Soto's syndrome, growth hormone insufficiency and premature sexual maturation.

Disproportionate short stature

Many conditions and diseases can cause disproportionate short stature, which is probably a short torso with short limbs and possibly a skull which may be different in appearance. Some conditions have a primary bone disorder called skeletal dysplasia, achondroplasia being the most common. Hypochondroplasia is a similar condition but the abnormalities are less apparent.

Achondroplasia

During foetal and early development, cartilage develops into bone. For those children with achondroplasia, the rate of this change is disturbed, resulting in short bones and reduced height. Children have an average-sized trunk and short arms and legs. It occurs in about 1 in 20,000 births, affecting males and females in equal proportions.

Pupils with achondroplasia may exhibit the following characteristics:

- relatively normal torso and short arms and legs;
- large skull;
- straight upper back with a markedly curved lower spine;
- loose joints;
- lower legs can become bowed;
- low back and leg pains;
- normal intelligence;
- over-crowded teeth;
- reduced muscle tone;

- increased weight;
- frequent middle ear infections causing some hearing loss;
- breathing difficulties caused by a small chest, large tonsils and a small facial structure.

Causes

The main cause of PSS is considered to be a lack of growth hormones produced by the thyroid and pituitary glands. Chromosomal defects in girls with Turner's syndrome can result in changes in growth rates.

Achondroplasia is a genetic disorder of bone growth. It is caused by an abnormal gene on one of the chromosome '4 pair'.

Treatment

There is no specific treatment which can reverse the effects of restricted growth conditions. Hormone treatment can be used in some cases to improve growth rates. Pupils may receive input from a variety of health professionals, e.g. dieticians, physiotherapists, occupational therapists. Surgical options may also be considered including limb lengthening.

> *For further information contact:*
>
> Restricted Growth Association
> www.restrictedgrowth.co.uk
>
> Child Growth Foundation
> www.childgrowthfoundation.org
>
> Dwarf Sports Association UK
> www.dsauk.org

Educational implications

Not all pupils with restricted growth will have learning difficulties. Some pupils will be late in reaching developmental milestones, but ultimately overall development is usually normal.

Pupils with short stature may experience difficulties related to self-esteem, inappropriate peer expectations and physical access. The following are points which should be considered.

- Expectations: be aware that both adults and their peers should treat these pupils appropriately. Monitor playground behaviour.
- If limb-lengthening surgery is planned, please refer to the advice contained within club foot (Talipes) in Chapter 11.
- Seating: consider height of chairs and desks, height adjustable seating may be appropriate. Footblocks at tables will help.
- Position in the classroom: give consideration not only to a pupil's size, but also to possible sensory defects, such as hearing loss or visual impairment.

- Movement between lessons: carrying equipment and bags.
- Access to equipment and materials in practical lessons: consider positioning of equipment on the table in the room, size of stools and tables in Art lessons.
- Fine motor skills: pupils with short, stubby fingers may need adapted fine motor equipment, such as pencils and scissors. The aim should be to facilitate independent access to the school curriculum, using the minimum of adaptations and additional support. Consider ICT equipment for recording work.
- PE lessons: check with parents whether there are any restrictions on physical activities. Generally, contact sports and other high-impact activities, such as jumping, are not advisable. Pupils with achondroplasia should avoid gymnastics and contact sports because of the potential for neck or back damage, due to existing spinal stenosis (narrow spinal canal, particularly in the lower back). PE staff should be made aware of any contra-indications. The Dwarf Sports Association UK can give advice on teaching sporting skills in school.
- Use appropriate equipment, e.g. short-handled racquets, bats.
- Independence skills: making minor adaptations to the school and classroom environment can easily foster independence. For example, provision of:
  - a lower coat hook in the cloakroom;
  - a lower handrail on staircases;
  - a step near the toilet and wash hand basins, extended tap turners;
  - lower door handles, light switches, locks on toilet doors;
  - use of glass in lower sections of doors, to ensure visibility;
  - dressing aids, as prescribed by OT.

29   Spina bifida

Definitions

Spina bifida is a fault in the development of the spine and spinal cord which leaves a gap in the spine.

Myelomeningocele

The spinal column remains open along the spine. The membranes and spinal cord push out to create a sack in the baby's back. Surgery can close the defect but damage will already have occurred resulting in:

- partial or total paralysis of the lower limbs;
- bowel and urinary incontinence;
- loss of skin sensation;
- most babies will develop hydrocephalus.

Spina bifida occulta (hidden)

- The opening in the spine is covered in skin.
- A very mild common form: in the majority of cases it is of no consequence at all and no treatment is required.
- There may occasionally be bowel and bladder problems.

Spina bifida meningocele

This is the least common form and the protective membranes surrounding the spinal cord are pushed out between openings in the vertebrae. The membranes can usually be surgically removed and no further treatment is required.

Cause

There is no known reason why spina bifida occurs but possibly lack of folic acid.

For further information contact:

Association for Spina Bifida and Hydrocephalus (ASBAH)
www.asbah.org

Treatment

- Surgery as above.
- Surgery to treat hydrocephalus – placing a shunt.
- Therapies – physiotherapy and occupational therapy.

Educational implications

- Pupils with spina bifida will vary in both their physical and their cognitive ability according to the type of damage caused by their condition.
- Bladder and bowel control can be late; in some cases it is never achieved. Catheterisation and bowel management may be required.
- Pupils who have myelomeningocele spina bifida are likely to be wheelchair users, although therapeutic walking and standing with a walking or standing frame may be introduced into the physical management routine. Bowel and bladder incontinence are likely to be present.
- Many pupils with spina bifida also have hydrocephalus and will have a shunt in their brain to drain excess cerebral fluid. Hydrocephalus can result in a range of learning difficulties. Refer to page 54 for guidance.

An inter-disciplinary assessment will inform school of the individual needs of the pupil. The following are general points to consider:

- awareness raising of any medical needs through an Individual Health Care Plan;
- plan movement times to take account of restricted mobility necessitating use of a wheelchair or mobility aids;
- consider access issues relating to difficulty climbing stairs or accessing the first floor in a wheelchair – timetable on the ground floor where possible;
- the pupil may have difficulty sitting on the floor during carpet time and assembly;
- PE lessons may require differentiation;
- a physical management routine may need to be incorporated in the school day – by whom, when and where will it be implemented?
- plan for liaison time with outside agencies;
- budget for funding to release staff for training in the use of specialised equipment;
- if manipulation of standard classroom equipment is difficult, is specialised equipment or a compensatory approach required?
- reorganise positioning of equipment to aid independent access;
- support the pupil in the organisation of his/her personal effects such as the school bag;
- facilitate disabled toilet access with appropriate moving and handling equipment;
- plan for support assistants to assist with personal care issues taking planned and unplanned staff absences into consideration;
- ensure staff carrying out support for bladder/bowel incontinence, e.g. catheterisation, are appropriately trained by appropriate health professionals.
- plan carefully for out-of-school visits;
- include careful planning for work experience placements;
- home/school transport may be required.

Health care considerations for pupils with spina bifida

Pupils with spina bifida frequently have a loss of sensation below the site of their lesion and as a consequence do not feel pain.

Care should be taken when:

- assisting the pupil with transfers between wheelchairs and classroom chairs;
- supporting the pupil in assisted physical activities such as walking with a rollator;
- applying and removing orthoses;
- positioning the pupil near heat sources (radiators, water pipes, sunshine);
- using potentially hazardous substances in science and technology.

Support staff may be asked to monitor skin condition and pressure point areas for signs of skin change.

Some pupils with spina bifida may be bowel and/or bladder incontinent and will require support for personal hygiene issues. This may include catheterisation.

Pupils who have hydrocephalus and have a shunt fitted will require additional health care strategies detailed in an Individual Health Care Plan. Refer to Chapter 21, Hydrocephalus.

30 Spinal injuries

Definition

A spinal cord injury is damage to the spinal cord resulting in a loss or impaired function causing reduced mobility or sensation.

Tetraplegia (or quadriplegia)

Tetraplegia is a high-level injury which occurs as a result of a broken neck or injury to the spine in the neck area. It causes part or full paralysis in all four limbs and affects the chest muscles which can cause breathing difficulties.

Paraplegia

This is a low-level injury which occurs as a result of damage to the middle and lower back and causes paralysis to the legs and abdomen. The amount of remaining movement in the trunk and chest depends on the point of injury.

Causes

An injury to the spinal cord can be caused by accidental injuries, viral infection, cysts or tumours on or near to the spinal cord.

Treatment

- Hospitalisation for a long period following the trauma.
- Assessments by specialist services to provide equipment.
- Catheterisation to drain urine; sometimes surgery to by pass bladder/bowel.
- Physical management by physiotherapist and occupational therapist to achieve maximum functional independence.

For further information contact:

Spinal Injuries Association
www.spinal.co.uk

Educational implications (acquired spinal injuries)

Low-level injuries occurring below the waist are likely to result in the following physical difficulties:

- loss of mobility;
- bowel and bladder incontinence;
- susceptibility to pressure sores;
- reduced stamina.

High-level injuries occurring in the neck area are likely to result in the following physical difficulties:

- loss of mobility;
- bowel and bladder incontinence;
- susceptibility to pressure sores;
- susceptibility to autonomic shock syndrome (see below);
- reduced stamina;
  and
- loss or restriction in fine motor skills affecting:
  - self-help skills, e.g. eating/drinking/dressing/grooming;
  - recording skills.

It is unlikely that the cognitive ability of pupils who have sustained a spinal injury will be altered after the accident. Their learning will be significantly affected by reduced stamina and possibly problems relating to self-esteem.

Refer to Sections IV–VI on the following areas for possible strategies to deal with:

- accessing the building;
- mobility issues;
- planning out-of-school visits;
- accessing the curriculum;
- alternative recording strategies;
- dealing with emotional issues;
- writing an Individual Health Care Plan (IHCP);
- joint protection issues, which will require further advice from the occupational and physiotherapists.

Autonomic dysreflexia

This is an emergency condition requiring immediate attention. It can affect people with paralysis as a result of a spinal cord injury. It occurs when there is interference to the normal function of the autonomic nervous system. The Individual Health Care Plan should be very detailed and concise.

Symptoms can include:

- pounding headache (caused by raised blood pressure);
- slow heartbeat;
- high blood pressure;

- sweating above the level of injury;
- goosebumps;
- blotching of the skin above the level of the injury;
- restlessness, anxiety;
- flushed (reddened) face;
- tightness in the chest;
- cold, clammy skin below level of spinal injury.

Untreated it can cause seizures and bleeding in the brain which can be fatal.

Action to take:

1. Send someone to contact parents or carers.
2. If symptoms are giving cause for concern, ring for an ambulance before contacting the parents.
3. Keep the pupil in an upright position.
4. Try to identify the cause of the problem and deal with it if practical, e.g.
   - catheterise to relieve bladder pressure;
   - loosen clothing to reveal pressure sore or toenail problem;
   - remove any orthoses to check skin condition.
5. Observe closely to see if symptoms improve.
6. Pass accurate information to the paramedics.
7. Update parents/carers as soon as possible.

Section IV

Meeting the pupil's medical and physical needs

31 Staff supporting pupils with a medical condition

Guidelines for members of staff

- Any member of school staff may be asked to provide support to pupils with medical conditions, including the administering of medicines, although they cannot be required to do so.

- Headteachers should ensure that school staff supporting pupils with a medical need are appropriately insured and that staff are aware that they are insured to support pupils in this way.

- Administering medicines is not part of teachers' professional duties; however, they should take into account the needs of pupils with medical conditions that they teach, i.e. the medical needs, the educational implications and social and emotional aspects of the pupil.

- School staff who are required to administer medication, or carry out procedures related to a specific condition, should receive sufficient and suitable training and achieve the necessary level of competency before they take on the responsibility. The relevant health care professional should normally lead on identifying and agreeing with the school, the type and level of training required, and how this can be achieved. Parents or another member of staff are not sufficient.

- Training should be sufficient to ensure that staff are competent and have confidence in their own ability to support pupils, and to fulfil the requirements in an Individual Health Care Plan. They will need an understanding of the specific medical conditions, their implications and any preventative measures. It would be inappropriate to expect a member of staff to work with the pupil until they feel confident.

- Staff must not give prescription medicines or undertake health care procedures without appropriate training (updated to reflect any Individual Health Care Plans). A first-aid certificate does not constitute appropriate training in supporting children with medical conditions.

- Any member of school staff should know how to respond when they become aware that a pupil with a medical condition needs help. It is therefore crucial that all staff (including lunchtime workers, site managers, transport escorts etc.) are aware that a specific pupil may need care on some occasion. All staff should know the appropriate response to a particular pupil's emergency needs and therefore training over and above general first aid training will be required.

- Staff who provide support to pupils with medical conditions should be included in meetings where this is discussed.

- Supporting a pupil should not be the sole responsibility of one person. Partnership working between school staff, health care professionals (and where appropriate, social care professionals), local authorities, and parents and pupils will be critical.

- Arrangements for whole-school awareness training should be made, so that all staff are aware of the school's policy for supporting pupils with medical conditions and their role in implementing that policy.
- Induction arrangements for new staff should be made. The relevant health care professional should be able to advise on training that will help ensure that all medical conditions affecting pupils in the school are understood fully. This includes preventative and emergency measures so that staff can recognise and act quickly when a problem occurs.
- Continuing professional development provision opportunities should be considered.
- The school's policy should additionally set out arrangements for whole-school awareness training so that all staff are aware of the school's policy for supporting pupils with medical conditions and their role in implementing that policy. Induction arrangements for new staff should be included.

Source: 'Supporting pupils at school with medical conditions' (2014)

Template A: staff training record – administration of medicines

Name of school/setting	
Name	
Type of training received	
Date of training completed	
Training provided by	
Profession and title	

I confirm that .... has received the training detailed above and is competent to carry out any necessary treatment. I recommend that the training is updated.

Trainer's signature   _____

Date   _____

I confirm that I have received the training detailed above.

Staff signature   _____

Date   _____

Suggested review date _____

32 Individual Health Care Plans

Governing bodies should ensure that the school's policy covers the role of Individual Health Care Plans, and who is responsible for their development.

Individual Health Care Plans (IHCPs) will often be essential where conditions fluctuate or there is a high risk that emergency intervention will be needed. They will be helpful where medical conditions are long term and complex. Not all pupils will require one. The school, health care professional and parent should agree, based on evidence, when a plan would be inappropriate or disproportionate; without a consensus, the headteacher should make the final decision.

When deciding what information should be recorded on IHCPs, the following should be considered:

- the type of medical condition, its triggers, signs, symptoms and treatments;
- the pupil's resulting needs;
- the required medication – the dosage and possible side effects, and appropriate storage;
- other treatments – the times these will be carried out, an appropriate facility for these to take part, the equipment required;
- access to food and drink which is necessary to manage the condition;
- dietary requirements;
- environmental issues – e.g. crowded corridors, travel time between lessons;
- the level of support needed to maintain good levels of health;
- some children will be able to take responsibility for their own treatment but the level of supervision should be determined;
- specific support for the pupil's educational, social and emotional needs, e.g. how absences will be managed, requirements for extra time to complete exams, use of rest periods or additional support in catching up with lessons, counselling sessions;
- individuals to be entrusted with information about the pupil's condition;
- what to do in an emergency, including whom to contact, and contingency arrangements.
- some children may have an emergency health care plan prepared by their lead clinician that could be used to inform development of the IHCP.

Individual Health Care Plans should not be onerous but capture key information necessary to maintain the pupil's well-being. The complexity of the plan will depend on the severity of the pupil's needs. The plan should be available to everyone involved in the pupil's care but confidentiality should also be observed. Where the pupil has a special educational need described in a statement or EHC plan, the IHCP should be linked or be part of either.

Schools should make their own decisions about the format of their Individual Health Care Plan; however, a proforma from 'Supporting pupils at school with medical conditions' (2014) is provided on pages 93–4.

Proforma for an Individual Health Care Plan

Name of school/setting	
Child's name	
Group/class/form	
Date of birth	
Child's address	
Medical diagnosis or condition	
Date	
Review date	

Family Contact Information

Name	
Phone no. (work)	
(home)	
(mobile)	
Name	
Relationship to child	
Phone no. (work)	
(home)	
(mobile)	

Clinic/Hospital Contact

Name	
Phone no.	

G.P.

Name	
Phone no.	

Who is responsible for providing support in school	

Describe medical needs and give details of child's symptoms, triggers, signs, treatments, facilities, equipment or devices, environmental issues etc

Name of medication, dose, method of administration, when to be taken, side effects, contra-indications, administered by/self-administered with/without supervision

Daily care requirements

Specific support for the pupil's educational, social and emotional needs

Arrangements for school visits/trips etc

Other information

Describe what constitutes an emergency, and the action to take if this occurs

Who is responsible in an emergency *(state if different for off-site activities)*

Plan developed with

Staff training needed/undertaken – who, what, when, how often it should be renewed

Form copied to

33 Managing medicines on school premises

The governing body should ensure that the school's policy is clear about the procedures to be followed for managing medicines.

The following guidelines should be adhered to:

- Medicines should only be administered at school when it would be detrimental to a child's health or school attendance not to do so.
- Medicines should be prescribed in dose frequencies, where clinically possible, which enable them to be taken outside school hours.
- No child under 16 should be given prescription or non-prescription medicines without their parent's written consent – except in exceptional circumstances where the medicine has been prescribed to the child without the knowledge of the parents. In such cases, every effort should be made to encourage the child or young person to involve their parents while respecting their right to confidentiality.
- Schools should set out the circumstances in which non-prescription medicines may be administered.
- Schools should only accept prescribed medicines that are in date, labelled and provided in the original container as dispensed by a pharmacist. The exception to this is insulin which must still be in date, but will generally be available to schools inside an insulin pen or a pump, rather than in its original container.
- Instructions for administration, dosage and storage should be included.
- All medicines should be stored safely in an appropriate non-portable, lockable container. Only named staff should have access.
- Staff must not give prescription medicines or undertake health care procedures without appropriate training (updated to reflect any Individual Health Care Plans).
- Staff administering medicines should do so in accordance with the prescriber's instructions.
- Administration of medication should be witnessed by another member of staff and recorded appropriately. This should show what, how and how much was administered, when and by whom. Any side effects of the medication to be administered at school should be noted.
- Medicines and devices such as asthma inhalers, blood glucose testing meters and adrenaline pens should be always readily available to children and not locked away.
- Asthma inhalers should be in the pupil's proximity at all times (Key Stage 1) and carried by a Key Stage 2, 3, 4 pupil at all times.
- An emergency reliever inhaler can be kept by the school. To obtain an emergency inhaler and spacer, write to a local pharmacy, on headed notepaper (signed by

the headteacher) requesting the purchase of a Ventolin/Salbutamol Metered Dose Inhaler and a Volumatic Spacer (with mask).

- Pupils should know where their medicines are at all times and be able to access them immediately. Where relevant, they should know who holds the key to the storage facility.
- Essential medication should all be available when the pupil is off-site, e.g. on school trips.
- When no longer required, medicines should be returned to the parent to arrange for safe disposal. Sharps boxes should be available for the disposal of needles and other sharps.
- A child under 16 should never be given medicine containing aspirin unless prescribed by a doctor. Medication, e.g. for pain relief, should never be administered without first checking maximum dosages and when the previous dose was taken. Parents should be informed of any medication given.
- A pupil who has been prescribed a controlled drug may legally have it in their possession if they are competent to do so. To pass it to another pupil for use is an offence. It would be necessary to monitor its use.

Responsibilities

Parents/Carers have a responsibility to:

- tell the school that their child has a medical condition;
- give complete and up-to-date information about their child's condition;
- give information about the medicines their child requires during school hours and when taking part in visits, outings or field trips and other out-of-school activities;
- provide information about changes to their child's medication;
- inform the school if their child is or has been unwell which may affect the symptoms, e.g. symptoms worsening or sleep disturbances due to symptoms;
- ensure their child's medication is labelled with their child's name;
- provide the school with appropriate medication labelled with their child's name;
- regularly check medication kept in school to ensure there is an adequate amount of medicine available and that it is in date.

The administration of medication should be included in the Individual Health Care Plan.

Template B: parental agreement for setting to administer medicine

The school/setting will not give your child medicine unless you complete and sign this form, and the school or setting has a policy that the staff can administer medicine.

Date for review to be initiated by	
Name of school/setting	
Name of child	
Date of birth	
Group/class/form	
Medical condition or illness	

Medicine

Name/type of medicine *(as described on the container)*	
Expiry date	
Dosage and method	
Timing	
Special precautions/other instructions	
Are there any side effects that the school/setting needs to know about?	
Self-administration – y/n	
Procedures to take in an emergency	

NB: Medicines must be in the original container as dispensed by the pharmacy

Contact Details

Name	
Daytime telephone no.	
Relationship to child	
Address	
I understand that I must deliver the medicine personally to	

The above information is, to the best of my knowledge, accurate at the time of writing and I give consent to school/setting staff administering medicine in accordance with the school/setting policy. I will inform the school/setting immediately, in writing, if there is any change in dosage or frequency of the medication or if the medicine is stopped.

Signature(s)   Date

34 Access to buildings

Recent legislation

The Equality Act 2010 states that an educational provider has a duty to make 'reasonable adjustments' to ensure that disabled students are not discriminated against. These changes could include:

- *changes to physical features:* installing ramps to allow access to the building, classrooms;
- *providing extra support and aids:* (specialist training and/or equipment, e.g. appropriate seating, ICT equipment.

Changes to make buildings accessible should be in the 'Schools Access Plan'.

Accessing the building for pupils with mild physical disabilities, e.g. hemiplegia, short stature

The headteacher and school governors will need to undertake a site inspection with either the site access officer or health and safety representative and consider the issues listed below.

- Do all external and internal steps have grab bars for the pupil's use?
- Do all flights of stairs have handrails on both sides for safety?
- Are there any sunken mat wells that could be a trip hazard?
- Are all steps easily visible with a contrast between tread and wall?
- Can the pupil open all doors independently?
- Is the accessible toilet facility clearly marked and free of clutter?
- Is there an area, e.g. medical room, that can be used for a physical management programme?

Accessing the building for wheelchair-users

These additional questions relate to wheelchair-users.

- Does each subject area/building have at least one level entry door?
- If there are ramps already in situ, do they comply with the latest guidelines regarding angle of slope? Are they fitted with either a concrete lip and/or handrails to ensure safety?
- Are corridors free of clutter?
- Are all doors wide enough for wheelchair-users to get through?

- Is there clear access *into* all classrooms, e.g. no cupboards next to/behind doors restricting space?
- Do fire doors in corridors open easily?
  - If not, encourage pupils to ask the nearest person to open the door for them – this aids social skills.
  - Newly built schools/blocks are having electro-magnetic door-stops fitted which are linked to the Fire Alarm system.
- Are there short flights of internal stairs? Can they be ramped?
- How will upper floors be accessed? Is there a lift large enough to be used by wheelchair users?
  - If not, the use of a stair climber may need to be considered.

(a) Stair climber in use   **(b) Stair climber[1]**

- What procedure will staff follow in case of a fire when a pupil is above the ground floor?
  - If in doubt consult your local Fire Safety Officer.

Areas of concern, which are not easily remedied, should be noted by the headteacher or site access officer, who will then need to contact the SEN office for advice.

HM government document 'Fire safety risk assessment: means of escape for disabled people' (2007) gives guidance for the fire evacuation of pupils with physical disabilities. Schools should consult this document in order to compile a personal evacuation plan for each pupil: www.gov.uk/government/publications/fire-safety-risk-assessment-means-of-escape-for-disabled-people.

The local fire brigade could also be consulted for advice.

1 By kind permission of Advanced Stair Lifts UK

35 Mobility issues

The following are issues that need to be considered for pupils who are independently mobile, but have some problems, e.g. hemiplegia, short stature:

- Always ensure that mobility aids, such as sticks and rollators (walking frames on wheels), are to hand and not a trip hazard to other pupils.
- The pupil may need to leave class a few minutes early to avoid crowded corridors and stairs.
- If the pupil requires adult oversight for movement between classes, try to provide distance supervision. This allows the pupil to maintain and develop friendships and independence.
- If the pupil needs closer supervision on the stairs, ensure the support assistant walks *beside* the pupil not *behind*.
- It may be appropriate to give verbal prompts to hold the handrail and/or move one step at a time for safety.
- The identification of 'drop off' points or provision of a locker would reduce the amount of equipment/books carried by the pupil at any one time.

When planning an outing arrange a pre-visit to check the site, stairs, distances to walk.

Additionally, for pupils in wheelchairs:

- Ensure support staff know the most easily accessible route to all subject areas.
- Look at classroom layout – is there sufficient room to negotiate around the classroom or at least get to areas that the pupil needs to access?
- If appropriate, ensure support staff know the location of the lift/storage place for the stair climber and how often to charge it.
- Ensure that a sufficient number of staff are trained to use the stair climber to cover absences and that retraining is arranged at 6–12 month intervals to cover safety regulations.
- Ensure all staff are aware of the fire drill for that particular pupil, where the nearest fire exit is, and whether it is wheelchair-friendly.
- When planning an outing, again arrange a pre-visit to check the site and whether all areas are accessible to wheelchairs. If not, find out if there are alternative activities available.
- Timetable downstairs classrooms where possible, particularly for registration.
- Devise a timetable to indicate the changes of positions of equipment, e.g. specialist seating.
- Pupils with low levels of mobility should have a Personal Emergency Evacuation

Plan (PEEP), detailing procedures to follow in the event of the need to evacuate the building. Information in the government document 'Fire safety risk assessment: means of escape for disabled people' (2007) should be followed. This can be found at: www.gov.uk/government/publications/fire-safety-risk-assessment-means-of-escape-for-disabled-people.

Risk assessments

It is the school's responsibility to carry out risk assessments. Risk assessments are required when a potential hazard has been identified and measures are needed to reduce the risk of that hazard occurring.

Increasingly, health professionals are required to carry out risk assessments relating to moving and handling pupils. These can be used to inform an individual risk assessment within school.

When preparing a risk assessment related to supporting an individual pupil, it is acceptable to cross-reference the risk assessment and Individual Health Care Plan, to avoid duplication of work.

It is important that all staff, who regularly move and handle pupils who have physical difficulties, attend an appropriate Moving and Handling training course.

Schools should refer to the Health and Safety website www.hse.gov.uk and search for schools health and safety within the website.

36 Adapted furniture

The aim of using adapted furniture is twofold:

i) to provide and maintain a good working position.

For example, the pupil should always sit on a chair with feet flat on the floor, with bottom well back in the seat, back straight and head in the midline to ensure a stable base (see 'Classroom organisation', page 118).

A pupil who constantly leans to one side could possibly develop a curvature of the spine. Additionally visual perception might be affected by distortion.

ii) to ensure physical safety.

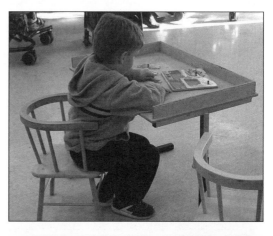

- A pupil with poor balance may require a chair with sides as well as a back.
- At Nursery/Infant level a small Captain's chair (seat height 28 cm) may be appropriate.
- To stop the pupil slipping forward in the chair put a non-slip mat on the seat.
- At senior level in subjects such as science, D&T, where the pupil would normally sit on a stool, either a science chair (right) or for more security an adjustable height 'perching stool' (left) covers the safety aspect.
- The pupil may also require an angled cushion to improve sitting posture and/or a foot block to ensure that feet are flat.

There are a number of commercially available foot blocks. These range from moulded plastic, which are generally used to aid toileting, to wooden stacking foot blocks which provide a choice of heights.

If the pupil's physical requirements are greater than those mentioned here, a full seating assessment by a paediatric occupational therapist should be requested.

Some pupils will require a different height of table at which to work.

- The simplest solution is to provide 'leg raisers' (to increase height), or some schools are happy to reduce the height of one of the tables already in a particular subject area, if a smaller table is required.
- Small mobile, adjustable-angled cantilever tables (see right) are fairly cheap, readily available and adequate for most situations. This would, for example, go over a wheelchair in any classroom environment.
- More substantial tables such as the Vari-tech 'Vari-table' would be more appropriate, e.g. in art, at secondary level.
- Additionally, there is a wide range of height-adjustable tables now available for both the secondary and primary setting. These may be used as standard classroom furniture for individual or groups of pupils.
- When planning for inclusion, secondary schools might also look at the range of specialised variable-height tables, available for use in ICT (see right), D&T, food technology (see 'Accessing Design and Technology', pages 135–8).
- For a pupil with a condition requiring careful positioning for posture and possible neck problems, the use of a copy-book holder or adjustable angle board for reading are beneficial.

37 Off-site activities

'Governing bodies should ensure that their arrangements are clear and unambiguous about the need to support actively pupils with medical conditions to participate in school trips and visits, or in sporting activities, and not prevent them from doing so. Teachers should be aware of how a child's medical condition will impact on their participation, but there should be enough flexibility for all pupils to participate.' ('Supporting pupils at school with medical conditions', 2014).

The following considerations should be made:

- A risk assessment should be carried out prior to any visit so that planning arrangements can take place. Health and Safety Executive (HSE) also gives guidance on school visits.
- Consultation should take place with parents and pupils together with advice from the relevant health care professional.
- The staff of a site to be visited, e.g. leisure centre, residential setting, should be informed of a pupil's condition to ensure the pupil is safe at all times.
- The following may be required:
  - suitable transport which has appropriate access for a wheelchair user;
  - good access to the buildings;
  - appropriate toileting facilities: an accessible space (a RADAR key may be needed) or a neighbouring school may offer a suitable facility, hoisting equipment, alternatives may be required (e.g. urine bottles), the pupil's intimate care needs (e.g. clean pads and disposal equipment plus staff requirements such as gloves, aprons);
- The Individual Health Care Plan (IHCP) should be taken which will include emergency contact numbers of parents and local hospitals, medication.
- If medication is required plans should include:
  - storage, locked cabinet, fridge;
  - dosage;
  - trained person and witness for administration;
  - recording of medication given;
  - emergency medication.
- The IHCP should indicate the need for extra snacks, drinks or alternative diets but guidance should be requested from parents.
- Lack of sleep or excitement can be a trigger for seizures.
- Accompanying staff who are trained to support the pupil's needs. For extended visits, staff will volunteer and cannot be coerced.
- The risk assessment will determine which activities are suitable for certain pupils and alternatives may be required.

38 Intimate personal care for pupils (guidelines for staff)

Duty of care

The **Children's Act 2004** places a duty on organisations to safeguard and promote the welfare of children and young people. This includes the need to ensure that all adults who work with or on behalf of children and young people in these organisations are competent, confident and safe to do so.

'Safeguarding children and safer recruitment in education', 2010 also encompasses issues such as pupil health and safety and bullying, about which there are specific statutory requirements and a range of other issues, e.g. arrangements for meeting the medical needs of children with medical conditions.

Intimate personal care

Intimate personal care includes hands-on physical care in personal hygiene, and physical presence or observation to support procedures during such activities. Some pupils may require support with personal care on a short, longer term or permanent basis due to SEN and disability, medical needs or a temporary impairment. This could include:

- pupils with limbs in plaster;
- wheelchair users;
- those with pervasive medical conditions.

Intimate personal care tasks can include:

- 'body bathing' other than to arms, face and legs below the knee;
- toileting, wiping and care in the genital and anal areas;
- dressing and undressing;
- application of medical treatment, other than to arms, face and legs below the knee;
- supporting with the changing of sanitary protection.

Guidance when supporting children and young people who require reasonable adjustments to be made in arrangements for personal care can be found under the relevant legislation, e.g. Early Years, Foundation Stage (2012), Equality Act (2010) and 'Supporting pupils at school with medical conditions' (2014).

The needs of the pupil will be part of the Individual Health Care Plan and a specific plan will be required to determine the exact requirements.

The following considerations should be made:

- the dignity of the pupil is maintained at all times;
- procedures are sensitive to their needs and preferences and their views are taken into consideration;
- the pupil should be able to give consent or withdraw from procedures;
- safety and comfort should be ensured during the procedure, e.g. the pupil should be on a safe changing place, access it with safety and correct moving and handling procedures should be in place;
- safeguarding procedures should be followed in order to protect the pupil from abuse;
- also staff should be protected from allegations;
- the pupil should be encouraged to care for themselves as much as they are able;
- the diversity of individuals and communities should be valued and respected and no discrimination should take place.

Facilities and resources

There must be suitable hygienic changing facilities for changing any children, the necessary resources should be included in a school's/setting's Access Plan. The Department of Health recommends that one extended cubicle with a washbasin should be provided in each school for children with disabilities.

Disposing of nappies/pads

Guidance from the Health and Safety Executive, 'Managing Offensive/Hygiene Waste' (January 2009), is that any disposal of waste for one child can be in the usual bins using appropriate nappy sacks. The waste would be considered to be municipal waste. For wet nappies a single bag is sufficient but soiled nappies require double bagging. Any more than this and schools will need to make special arrangements.

Agreeing a procedure for personal care in school

Intimate care in schools can be provided only by those who have specifically (either as part of their agreed job description or otherwise) indicated a willingness to do so. No employee can be required to provide intimate care.

Schools should have clear, written guidelines for staff to follow when changing a child so that staff are not put at any unnecessary risk.

Written guidelines should detail:

- who will carry out intimate care procedures (to include more than one person to cover for absence);
- where care will take place;
- resources which will be required and who will provide them;
- how nappies/pads etc. will be disposed of;
- how other wet or soiled clothes will be dealt with;

- infection control measures which are to be put in place;
- safeguarding procedures, e.g. what a member of staff will do if the child is unduly distressed or if marks or injuries are noticed;
- written agreements with parents about intimate care procedures;
- appropriate training for certain procedures, including catheterisation, colostomy care should come from health care staff and details included in the care plan.

Staff should take care (both verbally and in terms of their body language) to ensure that the pupil is never made to feel insecure.

Intimate care arrangements should be discussed with parents/carers on a regular basis and recorded on the child's personal care plan. The needs and wishes of children and parents will be taken into account, wherever possible, within the constraints of staffing and equal opportunities.

The setting/school should ensure that sufficient disposable resources are available, for example:

- antiseptic hand cleanser;
- paper towels;
- disposable aprons and gloves;
- nappy bags/sacks;
- cleansing equipment for infection control;
- disposal bin.

Parents/carers will provide:

- medical supplies as required;
- a supply of spare nappies/pads and wipes;
- spare clothes.

Off-site visits

Checks should be made beforehand to ensure that there are suitable facilities for intimate care available on excursions where they will be necessary and consider how intimate care can be dealt with in relation to PE, swimming, after-school clubs, transport to and from school etc.

Confidentiality

Parents and staff should be aware that matters concerning intimate care will be dealt with confidentially and sensitively and that the young person's right to privacy and dignity is maintained at all times.

For more detail see 'Guidelines for staff providing intimate care for children and young people' (2013).

An example of an Intimate Care Plan is provided on page 108.

Intimate Care Plan

Name of pupil	
Date of birth	
Address	
Name of parent/carer/guardian	Name of staff
Contact number	
Date written	Review date
Pupil's condition	
Where the intimate care procedure will take place	
How the pupil will travel there, e.g. walk, wheelchair – self-propel/adult oversight	
What equipment is required and where located	

Description of transfer method	
Adjustment of clothing	
Method of cleansing including washing hands	
Appropriate language, e.g. names for body parts and functions	
Number of staff, i.e. one or two	
Pupil participation, i.e. what can they do	
Disposal	
Next target towards independence	
Signature of parent/carer/guardian	Signature/s of staff involved with procedure/s

39 Physical management room

The following would, ideally, be included in a physical management room:

- a manual hoist or ceiling tracking hoists which enable a pupil to be transferred from one area to another without an adult lifting the pupil;
- access slings for transfers which vary in size according to the size of the pupil;
- transfer boards – straight or curved which enable the pupil to 'slide' across the board instead of using a hoist;
- a changing bed/plinth which is used when a pupil needs to lie down during any procedure;
- a toilet and in some instances a 'Closimat' toilet which cleans and dries the pupil;
- toilet frames which are positioned around the toilet and enable the pupil to stand and lower themselves onto the toilet;
- toilet seat reducers which are used when the toilet seat is too large or the pupil has poor postural security;
- footblock/s which support the pupil's feet when sitting on the toilet for better balance and security and/or to help the pupil get on/off the toilet;
- fixed grab bars which can be fixed onto one or two side walls so the pupil is able to hold onto them when getting on/off the toilet;
- drop down grab bars are fixed on the back wall and lowered/raised as required;
- a washbasin with lever taps so the pupil is able to turn them on/off easily;
- a hand dryer positioned so the pupil is able to operate it independently;
- shower areas in physical management rooms to enable a pupil to be showered with privacy with a shower seat for pupils who are unable to stand when being showered.

A physical management room is not for the sole usage of one pupil as equipment should be cleaned after usage and waste disposed of appropriately.

40 Toilet adaptations

Most schools now have a standard accessible toilet facility, but this may not meet the needs of all pupils. Different medical conditions have different toileting requirements which will need to be met within this facility. It should also be available for use by disabled staff and visitors.

Certain factors should be taken into consideration when planning to meet the needs of pupils with toileting difficulties.

Location

- Is the accessible toilet facility centrally sited?
- Is it available for the use of both sexes and well signed?
- Is the entrance free of clutter?
- Is it well lit, does it have independent heating and is it in good decorative order?
- Is the emergency light easily visible to passing staff?

Initial considerations

Even standard equipment may need to be adapted to suit individual needs, e.g.:

- lever taps are more appropriate for pupils with limited physical ability;
- an electric hand dryer is easier to use than a paper towel dispenser;
- the toilet roll/paper holder could be sited on one of the drop-down bars for easy access;
- a toilet seat insert and foot block may be necessary for younger pupils;
- if the pupil is able to use the same toilet facilities as the rest of the class, grab bars may be required for safety. N.B. mark the height with the pupil present to ensure the bars are in the correct position.

Range of use

Is the accessible toilet facility large enough to support the full range of medical needs?

Does it have a sufficient area available for nappy changing purposes?

- Nursery-aged pupils should be changed standing up, if they have standing balance. This protects support staff from developing back problems.
- For pupils who are unable to stand, a table (plinth) is more appropriate. N.B. A height-adjustable plinth is better for staff to work at than the static kind.

Are there wash-down facilities or space for these to be installed?

- A level entry shower is the best option, since this gives maximum potential usage.
- Shower controls should be height adjustable and the temperature regulated for safety and to encourage development of independent washing skills.

What are the disposal requirements?

- Products with normal body waste, e.g. nappies, can be double black-bagged and put into the usual school bins.
- Used catheters and colostomy bags can be double black-bagged and put in a dustbin.

Are there storage facilities for medical supplies?

- Are the upper cupboards the correct height for easy reach and safety?
- Is there a flat surface available on which to set out resources needed for semi-sterile procedures, e.g. changing a colostomy bag?

Additional requirements for pupils in electric-powered wheelchairs

- Is there room within the facility for the pupil to manoeuvre his/her electric-powered wheelchair?
- Is the door wide enough for easy access? Does the door open outwards giving maximum area for movement within the toilet?
- Is there sufficient space for the pupil, wheelchair and two support staff to manoeuvre within the toileting facility?

Pupils might also need:

- a commode, or moulded toilet chair, which should be assessed and prescribed by the paediatric occupational therapist;
- either a mobile, or ceiling track hoist, used with a sling, for transfers between chair and toilet/commode – this would normally be initiated by the paediatric physiotherapist/occupational therapist, who would advise and liaise as necessary with the company;
- the school would need to arrange equipment checks based on the recommendations of the suppliers after the first year's warranty is finished to ensure safety;
- staff would also need to be trained in ergonomic moving and handling to ensure that correct procedures are carried out – this would usually be arranged through the LA.

41 Introducing toilet training

Incontinence can be a part of a medical condition or can be part of a global delay. Some children will never be totally continent so the emphasis will be on management of the condition. Other children will be late in achieving developmental milestones and toilet training will be delayed accordingly.

A child will pass through three stages as they develop bladder control:

1. The child becomes aware of having a wet or dirty nappy.
2. He/she knows urination is taking place and may indicate this.
3. The child realises he/she needs to urinate and may say so in advance.

Toilet training will be more successful if the child is at the last stage.

Assess the child over a period of two weeks to determine:

- if there is a pattern to when the child is wet or dirty;
- the indicators the child is giving that he/she needs the toilet (actions, facial expression);
- hourly visits to the toilet and monitoring of wet, soiled or dirty nappies should help to determine toileting behaviour and show an emerging pattern.

Some strategies to support the process

- Familiarise the child with the toilets, use other children as good models (being sensitive to their privacy), flush the toilets, wash hands etc.
- Encourage the child to use the toilet when he/she is indicating in some way that there is a need, but do not force the issue.
- Take the child to the toilet at a time that the monitoring had indicated the child usually opens his bowels.
- Ensure the child is able to reach and is comfortable on the toilet.
- Stay with the child, talk to him/her, or take a book/toy to make the experience more relaxed.
- The child may not always use the toilet.
- It may take time to develop the idea of what is expected; don't become anxious.
- Praise the child when the toilet is used.
- There may be some setbacks (possibly an emotional reason), patiently continue.
- Accidents will occur – deal with them discreetly and without fuss.
- It may take time – be patient and success will be very satisfying.

It is important to develop a common home/school approach in order for the process to succeed.

42 Bowel incontinence

Some pupils with specific medical conditions may never achieve complete bowel continence. The parents or carers usually carry out most of the bowel management at home. This may include regular enemas and use of laxatives. Both parents and pupils need to be confident that any soiling issues can be dealt with discreetly in school whilst the youngster is working towards independent management of his/her condition. It is important that a common approach is used at home and at school with agreed strategies and rewards. It should be acknowledged that this can be a long process with setbacks along the way.

Consider the following points:

- sensitive sharing of information regarding the condition with relevant staff;
- access to a private toilet facility with waste disposal and washing facilities, but note that some pupils prefer not to use the 'disabled toilet' facility;
- arrangements to enable the pupil to leave the classroom discreetly, when necessary;
- arrangements to ensure a supply of clean underwear and wet wipes;
- access to drinks, as a regular fluid-intake is usually recommended;
- consider toilet arrangements for school outings – a RADAR key gives access to all public disabled toilet facilities. (Parents can contact their local council to buy a key for a nominal sum.)

Self-management in early years

- Emphasis should be placed on establishing a routine where the pupil checks his/her nappy/trainer pants/underwear, for signs of soiling at regular intervals. Initially, this should be on arrival, at playtime, before going home (for part-time placements), lunchtimes and playtime.
- The supporting adult should use a low-key approach, acknowledging when the pupil identifies correctly that he/she needs changing, but never showing disappointment that the nappy is soiled. Remember this is a medical condition and may not be in the pupil's control.
- Always encourage the pupil to get his/her own things ready. A pictorial cue card helps to establish this routine.
- Additional visits to the toilet will be required to deal with soiling incidents identified by smell.
- Nappies can be disposed of by double wrapping in plastic bags and placing in a bin, which is emptied by the caretaker in the usual way.

- Alternatively, a clinical waste collection service can be set up with the local council, who will arrange for a 'yellow bag' collection.

Self-management in Key Stage 1

- Building on the work done in Early Years, the pupil will be encouraged to initiate visits to the toilet at regular intervals.
- Consider use of a token system – the pupil places a token on the teacher's desk as he/she leaves the room to go to the toilet and collects it on return.
- The support assistant is not required to be in the classroom at all times. A system should be established whereby support staff can be summoned when necessary. Some schools use walkie-talkies to keep in touch and others use staff timetables to locate support staff.
- The pupil should be encouraged to take responsibility for as much of the cleansing and changing routine as is possible.
- Adapt the pictorial cue card to suit the pupil's reading ability/cognitive development.
- Gradually withdraw 'hands-on' support.
- Monitoring of progress by a member of the senior management team can be a good motivator.

Self-management in Key Stage 2

- Pupils should now be encouraged to implement their cleansing and changing routines independently, with oversight for emotional support and guidance. Some pupils respond well to using an alarm on their wrist-watch to alert them to the time to go to the toilet.
- It is hoped that independence will have been achieved well before secondary school transfer. Peer pressure plays an important role with older pupils, who become anxious if anybody knows about their condition.

Self-management in Key Stages 3 and 4

- Pupils generally manage their own cleansing and changing routines at KS3 and 4.
- Pupils should be given their own key to the designated toilet, if it is usually kept locked.
- It is essential that staff are sensitive to a pupil's need for privacy.
- SENCOs should ensure that a system is in place to inform temporary staff of any established routines, especially if a pupil needs to leave the room during lessons.
- Some pupils may experience emotional problems around puberty and can begin to deny that they have a problem. In a few cases counselling by a clinical psychologist may be necessary. Referrals can be made via the senior clinical medical officer (School Doctor).

My changing routine

Name:……………..………………………………..

Step 1: get clean pants ready

Step 2: use the wipes to clean up

Step 3: wrap everything in a plastic bag

Step 4: put the bag in the bin

Step 5: wash hands

Section V

Access to the curriculum

43   Classroom organisation

Arrangement of furniture

- Can wheelchair users enter the classroom without having to move furniture? Try to leave a clear access route to the pupil's desk.
- Is there a clear route for pupils with crutches or other walking aids to reach their desk? Encourage all pupils to keep the aisles clear of obstacles to enable pupils to leave the room easily and early to avoid the crowds.

Sitting position – good practice

- Does the pupil have a good posture when sitting? Try to encourage a whole class approach to monitoring sitting position. Aim for feet flat on the floor, bottom to the back of the chair, back straight, head in the middle.
- Place left handers next to each other to reduce arm conflict.
- Provision of a sloping writing surface can improve the working position and consequently the quality of handwriting. Consider the use of a commercial sloping board or an empty arch lever file.

Position of pupil in relation to teacher/board

- Does the pupil have any sensory impairment? If so, try to ensure they sit facing the teacher/whiteboard wherever possible.
- Place pupils with poor copying skills in the middle of the classroom – reducing the angle of eye-to-board-to-book movements. Avoid placing them at the back as they will have too many interfering movements between them and the board.

Copying from the board

- Avoid copying from the board if pupils have difficulty with visual perception. Provide teachers' notes from whiteboard presentations, pre-drawn diagrams which simply require labels.

General classroom resources/specialist resources

- Can the pupil reach equipment from his/her chair or when seated in his/her wheel-chair? Provide an individual set of equipment for pupils with limited mobility or restricted growth, so that they do not have to rely on help from others.

Deployment of support staff

Teachers standards 2012 states that teaching staff should fulfil wider professional responsibilities by deploying support staff effectively.

The SEND Code of Practice, 2014 states 'Where the interventions involve group or one-to-one teaching away from the main class or subject teacher, they should still retain responsibility for the pupil, working closely with any teaching assistants or specialist staff involved, to plan and assess the impact of interventions'.

The primary role of the support assistant is to facilitate independent learning. However, there are two main aspects of a support assistant's work which contribute towards supporting a pupil with a medical need or a physical disability.

Physical management issues – these may include:

- on-site access and mobility;
- personal hygiene routines;
- oversight in the playground;
- implementing a physical management programme;
- monitoring of seating position;
- administering medication and monitoring of medical supplies;
- checking and storing of specialist equipment;
- assisting with feeding;
- operating equipment, such as hoists and stair climbers;
- liaising with outside agencies, e.g. occupational therapist, physiotherapist and school nurse;
- developing independence skills.

Classroom/curriculum support issues:

- work on a 1:1 basis and in small groups;
- set up equipment, including ICT equipment;
- note key points;
- act as a scribe or amanuensis;
- give verbal prompting;
- organise worksheets and resources;
- support alternative recording strategies, e.g. dictaphone, photocopy notes;
- implement a speech and language therapy programme;
- developing independent working skills;
- carrying out physical tasks under the pupil's direction, e.g. Design Technology, Science;
- preparing differentiated materials under the guidance of the subject teacher.

General considerations

- The support assistant should be engaged in promoting independence at all times. It will not be necessary for the support assistant to work alongside the pupil in all lessons.
- The support assistant should take notes during curriculum delivery in order to reinforce key points at a later stage in the lesson. Care must be taken to allow the pupil to focus on the teacher and not the support assistant. Consider the support assistant's seating position within the room.
- The support assistant should work under the direction of the SENCO and individual subject teachers.
- In practical sessions, when the pupil requires support to manipulate specialised equipment, the support assistant should work under the pupil's direction.
- Communication with outside agencies should be noted and passed on to the SENCO.
- Withdrawal of pupils for physical management routines should be negotiated with the SENCO and individual subject teachers, with regard to subject and social issues.
- The support assistant may be asked to keep a written record to monitor the pupil in terms of stamina and physical performance. Home/school liaison should be established under the guidance of the SENCO/Head of Year.
- The support assistant may easily become isolated from the rest of the team if a high percentage of the support is given on a one-to-one basis. Be aware that support staff may require emotional support, especially if they work with pupils who have a deteriorating medical condition.

44 Alternative recording strategies

Pupils may experience writing difficulties for a number of reasons, reduced muscle strength, excessive fatigue and limited use of hand/upper limb resulting in poor letter formation and lack of fluency.

Initially, it would help to check the following areas, prior to remediation:

- sitting posture (see classroom management);
- pencil grip – is the pupil's grip unorthodox and tense? (see 'Specialised fine motor equipment', page 123);
- visual perception (check spatial awareness, body image);
- fine and gross motor co-ordination (check motor skill level, hand/eye co-ordination etc.).

The following strategies can be used to support those pupils with physical difficulties.

Primary level (Key Stage 1)

1. Teach the placement of letters on the computer keyboard using a drill and rote program (improves hand/eye co-ordination, upper/lower case letter matching and recognition).
2. Use word banks to create sentences/magnetic letters and numbers to create words in literacy and sums in number work.
3. Give the pupil work in 'cloze' procedure format, i.e. the pupil rings the correct word, or have a number of individual words from which they can make a selection.
4. Record the pupil's verbal attainment.
5. Record attainment through the use of ICT, e.g. on an iPad.
6. Act as the pupil's scribe, or arrange collaborative working sessions where another pupil does the writing.
7. Use the Clicker program, which requires only reasonable mouse skills to select words or letters. A wide range of grids is available to support many areas of the curriculum and new grids can be created very quickly and easily.
8. Provide the pupil with a numbers printing set for number work.
9. Use simple computer programs requiring selection by either space bar or the number line (consult the mathematics adviser if necessary).
10. Consider the use of 'big keys' keyboards, use of lower case keys. An alternative mouse may be needed.

Primary level (Key Stage 2)

1. Continue with 2–8 from primary level (KS1) if appropriate.
2. If competence is developing on the keyboard, investigate the possible use of a word processor for lengthy writing tasks. If you anticipate that the pupil will be reliant on a word processor at secondary level, teach touch-typing skills in preparation.
3. Encourage the pupil to continue to write small amounts with the emphasis on *quality* rather than *quantity*.
4. Give multiple-choice questions.

Secondary level (Key Stages 3 and 4)

As above but also:

1. Allow greater use of word processing to support homework, as well as work in school.
2. For pupils who are more physically disabled investigate drawing/CAD packages to support D&T modules.
3. Photocopy a friend's notes if extensive note-taking is required.
4. Provide the teachers' PowerPoint notes, giving the main points.
5. Continue to encourage the use of a 'Dictaphone' for homework.
6. Teach the pupil who has good spelling skills, but is simply slow at recording, to develop his/her own form of 'speed writing' using contracted words, e.g. prodd = produced, prodg = producing, prodn = production.
7. In Y10 voice recognition programs may also be considered if the pupil has good dictation and literacy skills that enable him/her to recognise mistakes and correct them.
8. Teach the pupil how to make more concise and effective notes or 'mind webs' to reduce the amount of writing required, e.g.

Not *this* –   **but this –**   **or this**

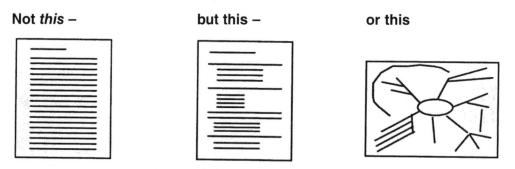

45 Specialised fine motor equipment

For those pupils who have difficulties in developing handwriting and manipulating standard classroom equipment, e.g. pencils, pens, scissors, rulers and compass, adapted equipment is available to promote skills and confidence.

To support the development of handwriting

The standardised tripod grip is not always the most comfortable for some pupils. However, the pencil grip must be relaxed and secure enough to allow them to produce a lengthy piece of writing.

A grip should be changed only if it is tense, looks uncomfortable and causes pain after writing for ten or more minutes.

Generally, pupils who wrap their thumbs or index fingers around the barrel of the pencil, have an *insecure* grasp and would benefit from remediation. One alternative is to hold the pencil between index and middle fingers (the Monk's grip).

Assess the pupil's pen/pencil grip.

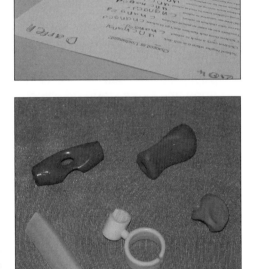

- Provide a range of pencils with different-sized barrels (including maxi and triangular) for pupils to trial.
- A selection of pencil grips should also be available – most schools have triangular grips available for use but often a moulded grip, which requires pupils to position their fingers correctly, is more beneficial.
- From the bottom left clockwise in this picture, you can see the standard triangular grip, the Tri-go grip, the Ultra pencil grip, the 'Stubbi' or 'Stetro' grip and 'Grip it' (used by putting the ring on to the index finger). Also try the 'Cross-guard' grip.
- A range of pens is also needed to try out – including gel ink pens as well as ballpoints, some with rubberised grips, since they each have a different 'feel' and what suits one pupil may not suit another.

- Sometimes the provision of an angled-board improves writing (see 'Classroom organisation', pages 118–20).
- To stop paper or books from sliding on the desk, use either Blu-Tack® or a rubberised non-slip mat.

Cutting skills

Low muscle tone or limited physical ability may result in poor scissor skills. There is a wide range of scissors now available for use. Classrooms should have a variety of scissors for pupils to select the most appropriate for their needs.

- The most difficult action is to open the scissors again once the pupil has completed the cut. 'Trainer' scissors (a) allow him/her to use both hands for cutting giving extra leverage.
- Alternatively an adult may guide the pupil placing his/her fingers in the first set of handle holds over the top of the pupil's hand.
- These scissors are all self-opening. From the left clockwise picture b shows the Peta looped scissors, Peta spring-loaded scissors and Fiskars nursery scissors. The pupil uses the whole hand to close the blades giving maximum leverage.

- These increase confidence, especially if a pupil has low muscle tone and struggles to open and close standard scissors using two fingers only.
- With practice the pupil may progress to using scissors that have a larger lower handle (c), thereby improving leverage.
- The scissors shown here are Fiskars Junior scissors and Hetty and Milly from the Berol range.

- Pupils with more severe physical difficulties may require 'table top' scissors (d). These are self-opening scissors, either mounted on a wooden or plastic block or resting on the lower horizontal bar.
- The only action required is to push down on the top horizontal bar.

Supporting number work

- Some pupils have significant difficulties handling standard number equipment, e.g.

Unifix™ cubes. These invariably end up on the floor, or the pupil loses count and does not develop a reliable counting pattern. This is simplified by using an abacus.

- When pupils begin to use a calculator they may repeatedly hit the wrong number. A large-buttoned calculator solves this difficulty.
- A large-buttoned scientific calculator can be found in the 'Accessories' menu within 'Windows' for those who need it.
- Additionally, there are a number of commercially produced, 'on-screen calculator' programs for computers that offer the facility of advanced calculations.

Other mathematics equipment

- Many pupils have difficulty using a standard ruler.
- Non-slip rulers can be found in a number of education catalogues. However, standard classroom rulers can be made non-slip by the simple addition of two small strips of 'self adhesive' Dycem™ (available from Nottingham Rehab or Homecraft) placed on the underside.
- A coloured sticker in the middle of the ruler also prompts the pupil to place his or her fingers in the correct position to draw a line. Holding the ruler at one end only, usually results in the other end being pulled down by the pressure of the pencil as it is drawn along it.

- For those pupils who have difficulty using a standard compass, the best alternative is the safe drawing compass, circle protractor or circle scribe. These can be used to draw circles of different diameters, the safe drawing compass also measures angles.
- A number of templates may be found in Art shops or catalogues to support lettering or design production for D&T or Art, e.g. for GCSE course work.

Science equipment

- Bug boxes that include integral magnifiers make it easier for the pupil to handle specimens.

- Use fixed magnifiers, e.g. the QX3 Computer Microscope, which can be linked to the classroom PC. This allows the pupil much greater control over the images and magnification. They do not have to lean over the desk to look down the microscope.
- Additionally, effective use of clamps and test tube racks, gloves, aprons and goggles to cover safety issues, together with non-breakable (Pyrex) test tubes/ beakers should be used.

Art

Try any of the following as appropriate:

- chunky crayons/pastels;
- thicker and shorter-handled paint brushes, including shaving brushes/decorating brushes;
- working at an easel or an adjustable-angled table (see 'Adapted furniture', pages 102–3) may be easier for pupils in wheelchairs;
- 'T-bar' brush holders;
- non-tip paint pots/holders;
- using clips/Dycem™ to keep work in place;
- printing with stamps rather than painting;
- Art/CAD programs to support design aspects;
- using 'clip art'/scanned images to support art modules;
- ICT – computer-based art programs may be easier for pupils to use in a more independent manner.

Textiles

- Provide large bodkins (metal or plastic) with bigger mesh materials.
- Embroidery hoops remove the need for the pupil to hold the material.
- Provide a needle threader.

46 Access to ICT

Pupils with limited physical ability, poor co-ordination, or low muscle tone may have problems using both the standard keyboard and mouse. Simply changing the settings in the 'Accessibility Options', 'Keyboard' or 'Mouse' menus etc. in the Controls panel may be sufficient to solve the problem.

Problems using keyboard	Solution
Pupil gets repeat letters/ deletions.	Turn off or slow down the 'Auto-repeat' feature. *Settings – Control Panel – Keyboard – Speed*
The pupil can hit a key accurately but cannot hit the correct key.	Make a card 'mask' to fit over the keyboard. Reveal the target letter/s plus the space bar, delete and return. Continue to reveal letters one at a time until the pupil can type their full name, then remove the mask.
The pupil has difficulty activating two keys at the same time, e.g. using the shift key to get a capital letter.	Turn on the 'StickyKeys' option, e.g. the pupil presses the shift key once and the next letter they select is a capital. *Settings – Control Panel – Accessibility Options – Keyboard*
The pupil has difficulty seeing the letters on the keys.	1. Raise the back of the keyboard, e.g. on a small angled board. 2. Purchase a set of yellow on black, or black on yellow stickers for the keys.
Problems using the mouse	**Solution**
The pupil has difficulty seeing the cursor on screen.	1. Increase the size of the on-screen cursor. *Settings – Control Panel – Mouse – Pointers – Select Option* 2. Turn on 'Mouse tails' (the cursor leaves a visual trail). *Settings – Control Panel – Mouse – Motion – Pointer Tails*
The cursor moves too quickly for them to control it.	1. Slow down the mouse speed. *Settings – Control Panel – Mouse – Motion – Pointer Speed* 2. It is also possible to use the number pad (all keys surrounding 5) on the keyboard to move the cursor – turn on Mouse keys. *Settings – Control Panel – Accessibility Options – Mouse*

The pupil finds it difficult to open programs using 'double click'.	1. Slow down the 'double click' speed. *Settings – Control Panel – Mouse – Double Click Speed* 2. Select the icon with a single click on the mouse and then press the 'Return' key.
The pupil finds it difficult to select menu/window options using the mouse.	Teach keyboard shortcuts, e.g. use the 'tab' key to scan through the menus, the up/down arrow keys to scroll through the options and return to select.
The pupil is left-handed or only has good use of the left hand.	Reverse the right and left button functions. *Settings – Control Panel – Mouse – Button Configuration*
The pupil has no hand function.	'Camera mouse' is a free resource developed by Boston College, USA. It enables control of the mouse pointer through head movements.

Alternative keyboards and keyguards

For those pupils who miss-hit keys, e.g. hitting two keys at once or may hit the key above/below/beside, etc., the use of a keyguard should be investigated.

These are made of plastic or, more frequently, metal and fit over the keyboard, usually attached by small pieces of velcro. The pupil can rest his/her hands on the keyguard and select the target letter through the correct hole.

There is a wide range of computer keyboards in use, all of which have slightly different dimensions, so a keyguard would have to be individually made to fit them. This can be costly and time consuming.

It is therefore easier and cheaper to purchase a keyboard and keyguard as a single unit.

Full-sized keyboards are available (top right).

However, there are reduced-sized keyboards, e.g. the 'Cherry' keyboard or the AlphaSmart (seen with optional keyguard). This may be used as a personal word processor, or for keyboard emulation linked to a PC if required.

For pupils whose *range* of movement is very limited, or who may require a more discreet word processor, smaller keyboards are available.

Touch screen monitors/tablets may be easier for a pupil to interact with. Apple 'iPad' has a large number of 'apps' that assist independent learning.

Some pupils require a keyboard with much larger keys, e.g. the Jumbo Board available in upper or lower case (a).

For those pupils who need a keyguard the Big Keys range has an ABC keyboard as well as the standard QWERTY layout. These are available with or without keyguards. A keyboard glove can also be purchased if required.

Big Keys LX has punctuation keys, which are not on the entry level Big Keys keyboards (b).

Pupils may also be unable to use a standard mouse effectively despite practice.

Trackerballs (c), which are available in all shops and catalogues, provide greater control. The pupil can operate the trackerball with one hand and press the selection button with the other.

Trackerballs may be simple and relatively cheap (see right).

However, if the pupil has a greater physical difficulty, the Penny and Giles Rollerball or Joystick (d) may be the best option.

These have a latching button at the top that requires a one press activation. A second press releases the 'drag' effect.

Both of these mouse emulation devices are now available with switch sockets to replace the left/right and drag button activation.

It may be necessary to request advice from the paediatric occupational therapist regarding the best positioning of equipment, especially for those pupils with a limited range of movement.

47   Accessing the PE curriculum

The National Curriculum acknowledges the entitlement of all pupils to a broad and balanced PE programme that will help to develop their motor competence and confidence, in both physical and social skills.

- The National Curriculum suggests that wherever possible, disabled pupils should be educated alongside their able-bodied peers without altering the activity.
- Where this is not possible, altering the rules or modifying the equipment should make the activity accessible. An *alternative* activity should only be offered if *modification* is not possible.
- If an *alternative* activity is offered, it should provide an educational experience and must not be a trivial or demeaning activity for the pupil.

One-to-one work with a teaching assistant should only be provided as a last resort; small group work with peers is more appropriate.

The following information should be gathered and taken into consideration when planning activities:

1. Specific information about how the pupil is affected by his/her condition.
2. Activities that have been recommended by the doctor or physiotherapist.
3. Contra-indicated activities, those that must not be attempted for medical reasons.
4. Special considerations related to the condition, e.g. the pupil with an indwelling catheter, with a urine bag strapped to the leg, would be more appropriately dressed in jogging pants, rather than shorts.
5. Availability and deployment of additional adult support.
6. Level of independence skills such as dressing/undressing.

General considerations

- Consider the disabled pupil during the planning and introductory part of the lesson. Ask the pupil for his/her opinion. Ask the class for ideas about how the activity could be modified to include everybody.
- Consider the language used, e.g.
  - send and receive instead of *throw* and *catch*;
  - *travel* instead of *run*;
  - *travel with ball* instead of *dribbling*.
- Consider including the disabled pupil in the skill element of the teaching session, but provide a modified 'small group' activity during team games.

130

Hockey

- Where possible, feet or wheelchair footplates can be used instead of hockey sticks.
- The use of Unihoc sticks on a hard surface enables most active pupils in wheelchairs to participate. If necessary, sticks could be attached to wheelchairs, so that the pupil has to manoeuvre the chair in order to hit the ball.
- Mark out a tackle-free zone or a 'no go' area in front of the goal to help unsteady pupils to play goalkeeper and be fully involved in the game, without worrying about being knocked over.
- Give pupils defined areas of play to ensure that slower pupils get an opportunity to play the ball and are able to do so, without the threat of being knocked.
- If pupils are playing in wheelchairs, it is important that sticks are not raised above knee height.

Netball

- Insist that all team members must touch the ball before attempting to shoot.
- Chalk a circle on the ground in the shooting area. To score a goal, bounce the ball in the chalked circle.
- Reduce the goal height.
- Provide a partner or 'buddy' for the disabled pupil who can catch the ball and feed it to his/her partner;
- Low-level floor 'baskets' are available commercially, e.g. www.livingmadeeasy.org.uk.

Football

- Allow pupils to use sticks or crutches to hit the ball.
- Create extra positions that will not involve too much running.
- A 'no go' area in front of the goal can help unsteady pupils to play goalkeeper and be fully involved in the game without worrying about being knocked over.
- Give pupils defined areas of play to ensure that slower pupils get an opportunity to play the ball and are able to do so without the threat of being knocked.
- Provide an oversized ball which will not get trapped underneath footplates, if a wheelchair-user is playing.

Rounders/cricket

- Use a larger or softer ball. The ball can be hit with a larger bat, stick, feet or wheelchair. 'Tee' ball is a variant of this idea.
- Provide alternative starting positions, e.g. balancing the ball on a cone, so that the disabled pupil can aim and hit, without having to cope with a bowler.
- Rounder runs can be scored by:
  - shortening the running area, e.g. arriving at second or third base;
  - having an extra post for the pupil to travel to;
  - making the fielders remain still for a count of 5, after the ball has been hit;
  - allowing powered-wheelchair users to use hockey sticks when fielding;
  - a 'runner' could be used.

Athletics

- All throwing events can take place from standing/seating positions. Someone should hold wheelchairs to ensure that they do not tip over. When throwing, wheel-chairs should be sideways on to the throwing area.
- Bean bags, wellingtons, tennis balls or clubs can be thrown instead of shots or discus.
- Javelins and bean bags can be directed to land on targets (precision events).
- Running and walking events, together with wheelchair dashes, 800m, 1500m races, are all suitable events.
- Wheelchair and electric wheelchair slalom courses are easy to set up, using skittles/cones.
- Pupils who participate in wheelchairs can be involved in measuring and recording the length of their 'jump', a jump being performed by a single push of a wheelchair between a marked set of tramlines.
- When hurdling, one is required to travel up and over an obstacle. The use of 'sleeping policemen' (preferably constructed of wood) will enable pupils partici-pating in wheelchairs to go up and over an obstacle.
- Swimming may provide pupils who cannot experience travelling distances over land with an appropriate and meaningful alternative activity.

Racquet games including tennis and table tennis

- Co-operative rallying games may be more appropriate than competitive games.
- Reduce the playing area.
- Operate a scoring system, whereby points are scored if the ball arrives within reach of the disabled player.
- Provide alternative 'tees', such as a cone, as an alternative to serving in tennis.
- Provide alternative bats – larger or lighter; experiment with Velcro straps to prevent the bat or racquet being dropped.
- Provide alternative balls, which are lighter or slow moving.
- Play without a net.
- Use table barriers to play 'side table tennis'. Lengths of plywood attached to the table, or PE mats leaning up against the table, keep the ball in the 'play' area for longer, thereby reducing the frustration factor.

Substitute activities

1. Snooker bowls

Bowls can be played on a snooker table. Each player uses two coloured balls. The game is started by the first player rolling the white ball to any spot on the table. The same player then rolls one of the coloured balls, trying to get it as near the white as possible, but it must rebound off at least two cushions. Alternative shots are then played and the player who finishes nearest the white, wins the 'end' and starts the next game.

2. Carpet bowls

These are played with 6.5cm (2.5in) diameter woods, obtainable from local sports shops.

3. Petanque

This is played with plastic or foam balls. The use of chutes (made from guttering) enables pupils with limited movement to participate.

4. Boccia

This is a simple form of bowls using light, pliable balls and a chute (see right).

5. Darts

It is possible to place the dartboard at a low level or on the floor. Safety dartboards are available with soft tip darts.

6. Skittles

These are played with plastic skittles and plastic or foam balls. Balls can be rolled, kicked or hit using bats or sticks.

7. Polybat

This is similar to table tennis and can be played on a table tennis table. The set includes eight side panels, table clips, an airflow ball and two polybats (see right).

8. Orienteering

School-based orienteering courses should follow a wheelchair-friendly route.

9. Fitness programme

Specific fitness programmes, designed to prove knowledge of good fitness habits for future life, should be devised. These should include advice from the physiotherapist, if appropriate.

10. Circuit training

Weight-training/circuit-training programmes could be arranged for older pupils.

10. Wheelchair-proficiency work

ROSPA provides a graded wheelchair proficiency training programme.

11. New age kurling

12. Refereeing and coaching courses

These could enable pupils to take active roles in their favourite sport.

Sainsbury's school games www.yourschoolgames.com is aimed at enabling participation in regular competitive activity and has the inclusion of disabled pupils at its heart.

Sainsbury's Active Kids for All http://inclusivepe-eng.co.uk has an Inclusive PE training programme for teachers.

See www.topsportability.co.uk for activities, e.g. zone hockey, table cricket and sitting volleyball. This website was developed by York Sports Trust to provide lesson plans and ideas/strategies to develop inclusive sports practices. In three sections: 1. Theories and background to inclusion. 2. Inclusive games – information re games developed to promote disabled participation. 3. Adapted/modified standard sports to assist inclusion.

48 Accessing Design and Technology

Points to consider when differentiating the Design and Technology curriculum to include pupils with physical difficulties:

1. Set finely graded specific objectives, e.g.

   - to be able to select equipment for measuring and marking wood;
   - to be able to give accurate instructions to TA to facilitate cutting wood.

2. Consider deployment of support staff for each activity, e.g.

   - support staff to work with an individual pupil or a small group of pupils;
   - support staff to modify/enlarge/simplify class work sheets.

3. Agree recording strategies with support staff, which will inform your assessment of pupils' work:

   - brief written notes by the support assistant can enable teachers to have an accurate record of support given in each lesson.

4. Ensure all practical work is pupil led:

   - when support staff are assisting with practical tasks the support assistant must work under the direction of the pupil.

5. Assess work using the same criteria as for other pupils:

   - if a pupil has given correct instructions to their support assistant, then credit them for their knowledge and understanding.

6. Consider classroom organisation and equipment storage:

   - a wheelchair user will require a workbench of an appropriate height;
   - an individual tool set will minimise movement within the classroom;
   - make other pupils aware of safety implications of a pupil working in a wheelchair; the wheelchair user is vulnerable at this height.

7. Consider special arrangements for examinations:

- pupils with additional physical needs are entitled to have the same assistance in examinations as they have in lessons;
- these arrangements can include a practical assistant, additional time, use of an amanuensis, rest periods and separate facilities;
- further details are available from individual examination boards on the QCA website and 'GCSE Examinations: Implications for candidates with cerebral palsy and associated disabilities', Scope Advisory Assessment Service (updated annually).

8. Consider working out of key stage:

- pupils may work from the programmes of study of a lower key stage to enable them to progress and demonstrate achievement;
- work should be presented in a context suitable to a pupil's age.

No-cost/low-cost adaptations – food

- Ensure at least one set of equipment is stored at an accessible height.
- Provide a perching stool if the pupil is standing for prolonged periods or if balance is a problem.
- Request advice from the occupational therapy service regarding use of standard equipment.
- Seek advice from the relevant educational support service regarding specialist equipment.

Pupils who have good use of one hand can use the auto chopper instead of a knife to chop vegetables.

Damp tea towels can help to stabilise a mixing bowl. Dycem™ non-slip mats are useful for anchoring a range of equipment. They are available in two thicknesses. Thick mats are useful for trays, chopping boards and heavy mixing bowls. The thin variety is supplied on a roll and can be cut to size.

The knob turner can be used for turning taps or knobs on a cooker. It comprises a series of retractable metal pins that mould to the shape of the object, providing a firm grip. This would be useful for pupils who have limited hand strength or reduced grip resulting from arthritis.

136

The sandwich spreader board hooks over the edge of the table and enables pupils to spread butter using one hand.

Vegetable holding boards are available which incorporate a grater and spikes to hold a vegetable whilst peeling it.

The kettle tilt can be used to ensure safe pouring of hot liquids. They are available in a variety of shapes and can be used to hold jugs and teapots.

A useful safety tip: encourage pupils who have tremors to stand their receptacle on a tray; if there are any spills they won't go on the floor.

A panhandle holder allows pupils to stir without holding the panhandle.

Medium-cost adaptations – food or resistant materials

- Use electrical equipment that duplicates a manual function, e.g. food processor for chopping vegetables, rubbing-in method for pastry, creaming sugar and fat for cakes.

- Use a mounting system for handheld electrical tools. These may need to be designed and made by D&T technician.
- Use commercially available clamps to stabilise work when marking and cutting.
- Provide an individual set of tools, possibly lightweight or junior versions, to be used by pupils with low muscle tone or weakness in their hands.
- Investigation is recommended for specialist equipment through specialist catalogues such as Nottingham Rehab or Smith and Nephew Homecraft.

Higher-cost adaptations

Use height-adjustable furniture and height-adjustable workstations including hob and sink to provide access for all pupils.

Pupils with short stature, those in wheelchairs and those in standing frames could benefit from access to a height adjustable sink.

Wall-mounted, built-in oven with pull-out tray will protect the wheelchair user's legs.

A combination microwave oven on an accessible work surface would negate the need for an oven.

Leave an open kick board space to allow for wheelchair footplates.

Pull-out storage racks in cupboards are easy to access.

Section VI

Developing skills for learning

49 Developing visual perception

Pupils with perceptual difficulties tend to bump into objects or people, have a poor understanding of the 3D world and its relationship to 2D pictures, and have problems acquiring the skills of reading and writing.

Classroom support for pupils with problems with visual perception

Staff should be aware that pupils demonstrating problems with visual perception may:

- have difficulty copying from the board;
- be slow at reading and, therefore, reluctant to read aloud;
- find small text difficult to read;
- miss out words/lines when reading;
- have difficulties reading text in different fonts;
- have problems developing handwriting.

There are a variety of ways to support pupils in the classroom:

- Provide a quiet area, which is clear of decoration/stimulus, for the pupil to work in.
- Reduce visual clutter in displays.
- Provide simple, clear work sheets and activity cards.
- Enlarge text and use double spacing.
- For some pupils print work sheets on a coloured background to reduce the 'glare' of white paper.
- If the pupil has to do a drawing, give him/her a frame to work within (helps contain work and aids positioning on the page).
- Give a pre-drawn diagram to label if drawing is very difficult.
- Seating position in class is important. The pupil should sit facing the whiteboard and teacher (not at an angle to it, since this distorts visual perception) for all copying work.
- Using a fixed-angled board also helps since there is reduced eye movement between model and reproduction.
- When writing allow the pupil to write on alternate lines since this reduces visual clutter.
- Holding a book upright when reading reduces visual distortion of text.
- Point to each word or use a piece of card, or a ruler, to highlight the line being read.
- The pupil may need to work through 'Write from the Start', a perceptuo-motor program that helps all the areas of skill development required to aid writing.
- Consider the use of ICT as an alternative recording method.

Problems with:	Try the following:
Spatial organisation difficulties (i.e. visuo-spatial awareness) **Check:** Does the pupil have a good understanding of positional words, up, down, in front of, behind, above, below, between, beside? Can he/she move forwards, backwards, sideways, clockwise, anti-clockwise, to the right/ left, on request?	Begin with gross motor activities (movement through space): • make obstacle courses (increase difficulty), slalom courses, mazes (ask the pupil to verbalise moves), team games. Then hand/eye co-ordination tasks (reduced movement in limited space): • threading/lacing/pegboard patterns/ building with Lego; • when beginning writing, put a finger or space template between words.
Form constancy The understanding that an object stays the same regardless of position in space, e.g. reducing in size in the distance.	• matching pairs; • shape recognition/classification by shape, colour, size, etc.; • ring the odd one out, same/different; • use small cut-out shapes to create bigger shapes/pictures (using a template to begin with, then without); • copy a shape/complete the drawing of shape or object.
Orientation and laterality Reversals seen (left/right, top/bottom). **Check:** Eye dominance – if the pupil has cross-laterality, i.e. right-handed and left eye dominant, he/she may experience the following problems: • developing left/right orientation on the page; • reversals of letters or words; • mixing left and right sides of the body; • be slow to develop hand dominance.	Use a multi-sensory approach: • involve touch and sight using three dimensional letters; • give visual perception exercises, e.g. ring all the letter 'b's; • have one pupil write a letter on the back of another pupil, who should identify the letter – get him/her to talk through the movements as he/she is forming them; – **N.B.** 'up' and 'down' have more relevance in this situation because of the vertical position for the activity; • use 'word play' prompts, e.g. bat and ball (for 'b').
Figure/ground discrimination (problems with focus resulting from too much visual stimulus).	• mosaics, inset boards, jigsaws, etc.; • pick out/colour/objects in busy pictures; • play spot the difference; • recognise an object/picture as it is gradually revealed.

50   Developing memory skills

To develop short- and long-term memory skills:

- Provide a list of topic/subject-related words at the onset of each term – this helps parents to know what is going to be covered, it helps pupils who take time assimilating new vocabulary and provides material for spelling development.
- Provide coloured pens/encourage use of coloured pens – colour helps stimulate visual memory, improves clarity of notes, highlights key words and word associations. These are fun to use and this encourages reluctant writers.
- Create summary cards of topic material when each topic is completed, to aid over-learning and revision.
- Provide wall displays of key terminology to help those with weak spelling and/or weak word association skills.
- Encourage pupils or support staff to write key words on individual Post-it® stickers. These can then be arranged in an appropriate order and discarded when used.
- Maintain the use of a planner/diary to help the pupil remember specific items.
- Consider sound levels in classroom. Background hubbub can be extremely distracting for some pupils. Background music can help screen out background noise and can aid concentration.
- Ensure pupils know the purpose of tasks, particularly homework. This can help them focus on appropriate factors.
- Beware of overloading the working memory. Pupils with reading, listening, spelling and writing difficulties are easily overloaded, leading to confusion, frustration and reduced transference to long-term memory.
- Encourage use of 'mind-maps' for each module of work, to give an overview of work covered and to aid revision or over-learning.
- ICT games, e.g. www.bbc.co.uk/scotland/brainsmart/games; memory boosting games www.learninggamesforkids.com.

51 Promoting attention and listening skills

Some pupils may have poor attention and listening skills related to their medical condition. The following suggestions should be considered:

- Play listening games:
  - www.busyteacher.org 'Do you hear what I hear? 8 activities to improve listening skills';
  - ICT games, e.g. www.bbc.co.uk 'Stimulus sounds' – games for encouraging listening skills.
- Say the pupil's name first and gain his/her attention before giving instructions or information.
- Ensure instructions are at the pupil's level of understanding, e.g. two/three word level of understanding.
- Try ICT, e.g. www.mdel.com – interactive listening activities.
- Ensure work is at the appropriate level, differentiated to the pupil's level.
- Assess how many instructions the pupil can follow and use cue cards to give a pictorial prompt for the sequence of actions required in an activity.
- Give time for the pupil to process the information.
- Reduce visual stimulation around the pupil's workspace and ensure that it is away from the window, displays, etc.
- Remove distractions, e.g. objects on the desk which can be fiddled with instead of listening. Alternatively provide a material which can be manipulated without causing a distraction, e.g. Blu-Tack™.
- Seat the pupil near to the teacher in order to promote good listening and attention skills. Use a visual signal to give reminders.
- Set tasks which match the pupil's ability to concentrate on a task. Work on extending his/her concentration span in the pupil's IEP.
- Younger pupils can be involved in activities to develop listening skills:
  - simple lotto games matching everyday objects which make sounds to pictures, e.g. the adult squeaks a plastic duck behind their back and the child matches it to the appropriate picture;
  - following actions in rhymes;
  - playing games such as 'Simon says…'.

52 Developing organisational skills

Some pupils will need support to develop organisational skills. Others may need strategies to overcome difficulties. The following are suggestions that may help:

- Provide a method of showing the structure of the day through a visual timetable, diary.
- Give pictorial task cards to aid organisational skills, e.g. a card to show in which order clothes should be put on when dressing after PE, prompt cards to indicate equipment needed for a lesson, or have a mat with templates of the equipment which is needed for an activity.
- Some pupils may need extra support to organise themselves in class, e.g. at tidy-up time, after group input, by receiving extra instructions in a simple manner.
- Help the pupil to develop organisational skills by providing cue cards for different activities, individually or on a flip chart for a group of pupils:

For this activity you will need your:

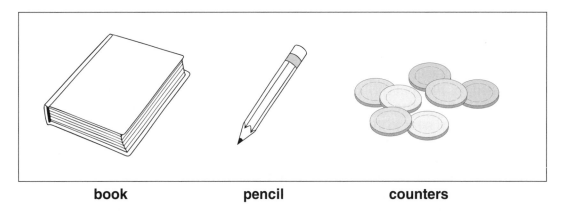

| book | pencil | counters |

- Encourage parents to make their child's belongings more easily distinguished by the use of a particular logo or colour, clearly labelled with his/her name.
- Encourage parents to buy school bags with different compartments to enable each one to be used for a different organisational function, e.g. PE equipment, dinner money, subject wallets.
- Differentiate subjects by colour, match to colour spots on the timetable, back text books in a colour to match the subject.
- Use clear plastic wallets to pack equipment for each subject, colour-matched, which may result in duplication of equipment but make for simpler organisation at the beginning and end of each lesson, e.g. pen, compass, ruler, calculator in a maths wallet.

- Ensure the pupil has noted homework requirements in some form, e.g. teacher noting work, use of a Dictaphone™.
- Use a home/school diary to encourage equipment and homework to be brought to school at the correct time.
- Suggest to parents that they encourage their child to develop organisational skills at home by having a white board near the door, with reminders of what is needed when packing their bags the night before.
- Pupils may need support for organisation at lunch time, e.g. collecting a lunch tray whilst carrying a bag and then finding a seat.
- Use a plan of the school to help movement around the site.
- Locker or designated place to leave equipment and reduce the carrying load.

53 Supporting emotional issues

There are a large variety of emotional issues related to medical conditions and these are also interlinked with issues of self-esteem and establishing positive peer group relationships.

Issues which may arise	Strategies and practical help
frustration at restrictions brought about by the condition, e.g. not being able to participate in sports	• allow discussion of frustrations with school staff and ensure that the pupil has access to as many activities as possible within the limitations of his/her condition; • look for alternative activities.
instances of bullying or teasing	• ensure that the pupil's concerns related to bullying and teasing are addressed; • use circle time as a forum for raising and addressing the issues of bullying and teasing; • consider the use of 'circle of friends'.
depression, resentment, anger; anxiety about the condition; appearance of new symptoms; recurrence of symptoms; feelings of being 'different'.	• ensure the pupil has access to a professional, e.g. a member of staff or specialist nurse, who can discuss the issues related to the condition; • ensure regular feedback to parents.
the need for permanent medication and treatments can be a dominant factor	• enable the pupil to regard treatments and medication as an accepted part of his/her life, by dealing with it in a 'matter of fact' way; • provide easy access to treatment or medication, water, snacks and all other factors in the health care plan; • encourage the pupil to be open with his/her peers; • allow friends to accompany them where appropriate.

interruption of schooling through hospitalisation and treatments	• ensure the pupil is made welcome on his/her return; • encourage peers, e.g. the 'buddy' system, to help him/her back into normal routines; • consider how work that has been missed will be made up – teacher/ student notes being passed on, extra tuition.
embarrassment at some of the more obvious symptoms	• use occasions such as PHSE or circle time (if the pupil or parents are happy with this).
dealing with fluctuating condition – 'good days', 'bad days'	• encourage all concerned to have empathy, e.g. peers, other adults, and plan accordingly; • watch for indicators and reduce demands on the pupil accordingly; • encourage the pupil/parents to take professional advice; • encourage older pupils to be self-limiting.
feelings connected with deterioration in condition, e.g. grief, fear	• be prepared to engage in pupil-led discussion, being sensitive to the level of understanding, depth of questioning and parental wishes; • recognise that it may not be possible to answer all the questions; • provide a place in school where the pupil can have some 'space'.
death of a peer with a similar condition	• all adults concerned with pupils facing deteriorating conditions, should have access to support, further information and training, e.g. Lost for Words training (see over); • when another pupil with the same condition dies, anticipate that the pupil will exhibit emotions and may wish to talk, cry or be given space to deal with this in his/her own way; • allow friends to find a way of supporting each other.
being over-burdened by other people's emotions, i.e. parents, peers, teachers, etc.	• try to provide as normal a routine as possible; • give an explanation to the class, when the pupil is not present.

Be aware that many of the issues may be relevant to other pupils in the class who may need reassurance, explanations and support.

School staff will require training for issues related to pupils with medical conditions in order to support pupils in their care.

Staff will not always feel that they have answers but should be as sensitive as possible.

Further information

Coping with Bereavement: A handbook for teachers
John Holland
Cardiff Academic Press
St Fagans Road
Fairwater
Cardiff CF5 3A3
Tel: 01222 554909

Understanding Children's Experiences of Parental Bereavement
John Holland
Jessica Kingsley Publishers
ISBN 978 1 84310 016 4

Lost for Words
John Holland, Ruth Dance, Nic MacManus and Carole Stitt
Jessica Kingsley Publishers
ISBN 978 1 84310 324 0

Life and Loss: A guide to help grieving children
Linda Goldman
Routledge
ISBN 978 0 415 85389 7

54 Developing a positive self-image

A pupil who has a positive self-image will have the confidence to deal with difficulties related to their condition and be more confident in new situations. Schools should adopt measures, some of which are listed below, to promote such an image.

- Have a positive attitude to the pupil.
- Ensure that all staff are made aware of the pupil's condition, the implications and the considerations needed to meet the pupil's needs to enable the pupil to have a feeling of well-being.
- Meet the needs in an unobtrusive manner.
- Ensure the pupil's dignity is maintained, e.g. privacy is given if a seizure takes place or when receiving medication.
- Be sensitive to the pupil's needs and aware of their limitations.
- It may be appropriate to inform other peers of the pupil's medical condition (in accordance with the pupil's and parents' wishes) in order for them to have understanding.
- Close friends may play a role in supporting the pupil in some way, e.g. carrying a tray, accompanying between classes, passing on notes for lessons missed due to absence related to the medical condition, reporting a change in condition to a member of staff.
- Bullying and teasing should not be tolerated.
- Have an assigned member of staff as a 'listening ear', for those pupils who find this useful.
- Work should be at an appropriate level to the pupil, possibly addressed in an IEP, but not necessarily, as some pupils will not have learning difficulties related to their condition. Achievement will increase confidence.
- If self-esteem needs a boost, it may be useful to give some responsibility to the pupil, e.g. monitor, 'buddy'.
- Use displays as a way of celebrating achievement across the ability range.
- Ensure that pupils are not penalised for absences related to their medical condition, e.g. when class points are gained for attendance.
- Support peer group interaction if a long or frequent absence from school occurs, through social media (with pupil and parental permission).
- Encourage peers to welcome the pupil back to school after absence from school.
- Teacher assessment should be used for internal testing, if frequent absence affects attainment grades.

References and further reading

References

Fire safety risk assessment: means of escape for disabled people
HM Government 2007, www.gov.uk/government/publications/fire-safety-risk-assessment-means-of-escape-for-disabled-people

Teachers Standards: Guidance for school leaders, school staff and governing bodies
July 2011, Department for Education

Guidelines for staff providing intimate care for children and young people
May 2013, reviewed February 2015, Service Children's Education

Health and Safety website www.hse.gov.uk
Search for schools health and safety within the website

Special educational needs and disability code of practice: 0 to 25 years
January 2015, Department of Education, Department of Health

Supporting pupils at school with medical conditions: Statutory guidance for governing bodies of maintained schools and proprietors of academies in England
September 2014, Department for Education

Further reading

Dignity and Inclusion: Making it work for children with complex health care needs
Jean Carlin 2014, Council for Disabled Children

Templates

Templates: Supporting pupils at school with medical conditions
2014; templates on pages 90, 93–4 and 97 are taken from this document

ICT equipment

Big keys, lower case stickers, specialist mice, inclusive technology, SEMERC

Suppliers

List of suppliers	Tel. Number/Web/Email	Equipment
Advanced Stairlift (Scotland) Ltd Unit 3, Burnside Business Court North Road Inverkeithing Fife, Scotland KY11 1NZ	01383 411400 www.advancedstairlifts.co.uk	Stair Climber demonstrations
Bishop Sports and Leisure Bishop House East Burnham Park Crown Lane Farnham Royal Slough, Berkshire SL2 3SF	01753 648666 www.bishopsport.co.uk	PE equipment
Inclusive Technology Ltd Gateshead Business Park Delph, Oldham OL3 5BX	01457 819790 www.inclusive.co.uk	Equipment to support ICT
Innovations in Sport Davies Sport Excelsior Road Ashby Park Ashby de la Zouch Leicestershire LE65 1NG	0845 1204 515 www.daviessports.co.uk	PE equipment
LDA Duke Street Wisbech Cambridgeshire PE13 2AE	01945 463441 www.ldalearning.com	Fine motor equipment
Maudesport Beecham Close Aldridge Walsall West Midlands WS9 8UZ	01922 45957 www.maudesport.com	Special needs PE equipment

Nottingham Rehab Supplies Novara House Excelsior Road Ashby Park Ashby de la Zouch Leicestershire LE65 1NG	0845 121 8111 www.nrs-uk.co.uk	Ramps Cutlery, food preparation Adapted furniture, fine motor/PE/ Food Technology equipment Moving and handling equipment
ROMPA Ltd Goyt Side Road Chesterfield Derbyshire S40 2PH	0800 056 2323 www.rompa.com	Fine motor and PE equipment
SEMERC Granada Learning Ltd Granada Television Quay Street Manchester M60 9EA	0161 827 2927 www.semerc.com	Equipment to support ICT including computer trolleys
Smith & Nephew Homecraft Ltd PO Box 5665 Kirby-in-Ashfield Notts NG17 7QX	01623 721000 homecraft.sales@smith- nephew.com	Adapted furniture, fine motor, Food Tech equipment
Step by Step Lee Fold Hyde Cheshire SK14 4LL	0845 300 1089 sbs@stpbystp.demon.co.uk	Adapted furniture